A SEQUEL TO A VOYAGE TO BOTANY BAY

BY

GEORGE BARRINGTON

Edition : Culturea (culurea.fr), 34 Hérault
Contact : infos@culturea.fr
Impression : BOD, Norderstedt (Allemagne)
ISBN : 9791041981854
Date de publication : juillet 2023
Mise en page et maquettage : https://reedsy.com/
Cet ouvrage a été composé avec la police Bauer Bodoni

A Sequel To A Voyage To Botany Bay

Chapter I.

The long silence which I have observed, must have led my friends to conclude that I had relinquished all my European connexions,--that from some untoward accident, or the natural visitation of Providence, they would never hear from me more;--but that not being the case; after assuring them that it merely proceeded from the multiplicity of business, and the unceasing vigilance my situation demanded, I shall without farther preface resume my narrative.

The government of this colony now devolved upon Francis Grose, Esquire, Commandant of the New South Wales Corps. He immediately superseded the civil power at Parramatta by the military, and all complaints in future were to be preferred to the military officer on duty there. Hitherto the magistracy regulated all differences, and punished such offences as required immediate cognizance on the spot; reporting his proceedings, from time to time, to the governor; and every order emanating from his excellency, respecting the regulation of the convicts, was promulgated through the same channel.

At Sydney, similar regulations took place, and all reference to the civil magistrate was in future to be dispensed with. It had been usual with the magistrates to hold a kind of court weekly, or as often as occasion might require; and to inflict such punishment as they deemed proportionate to the offence, always reporting their proceedings, as before stated.

At this time the magistracy consisted of the Lieutenant Governor and the Judge Advocate, who were justices of the peace in virtue of their commissions; the Reverend Mr. Johnston, Augustus Alt, and Richard Atkins, Esquires, who had been sworn in as magistrates by governor Philip.

No inconvenience having arisen from the former mode of dispensing justice, the cause of the change cannot be easily accounted for; unless it were that prediliction military governors generally possess, of concentrating all the power in their own hands.

Governor Philip had gratuitously distributed among the settlers, stock of various kinds, for the purpose of breeding; but he was scarce out of sight of the settlement when the greater part was brought to market; when, had not the officers purchased the whole, his benevolent intentions would have been frustrated, by the greater part being prematurely consigned to the pot or the spit.

New regulations now took place in the working hours of the convicts,--the time of labour was fixed from five in the morning 'till nine, and then rested until four, when they resumed their work, which terminated at sunset. This was a very salutary alteration, as they not only avoided the scorching ray of the noon-day sun, but had an opportunity of earning a title for themselves, at their respective trades.

About this time a very serious calamity befel the settlement, the weather was excessive sultry, and the grass having been set on fire by the natives raged on all sides, whereby several of the gardens were destroyed, and I was in the utmost jeopardy of losing my little all.--The progress of the fire, by the efforts of the settlers at Parramatta and its neighbourhood, being checked, and nearly extinguished, but a spark lodging among the thatch of a house on the adjoining farm soon spread out into a blaze, and consumed the same, out houses & c. and it was only by the greatest exertions it was prevented from communicating to my premises.

From the arrival of several American Vessels, New England Rum now began to circulate in considerable quantities, the baneful effects of which were soon conspicuous, in the frequent intoxication of the convicts.--The fondness they evinced for this deleterious liquor was incredible; they would run any hazard to procure it, and preferred receiving it as the price of their labour, to any other article, either of provisions or cloathing.

To remedy this evil, the governor issued an order, wherein he stated that if it ever appeared that a convict was possessed of liquor, supplied by the commissaries, that he should consider them as responsible for any irregularities that might happen in consequence of such injudicious and reprehensible conduct.

A deplorable instance of the mischevous effects of inebriety now happened, Elenor Mc Cave, wife of Charles Williams, a settler, one of my neighbours, with an infant; and a Mrs. Green, was drowned returning to Parramatta from Sydney, where they had been spending the day, drinking and revelling; it blowing fresh the boat heeled considerably, and the woman, Green, getting up suddenly to move a bag of rice to windward, to prevent its getting wet, the boat upset, and the two women and child were drowned: the child was snatched from the mother's hold, who was sinking with it, and brought on shore, but for want of proper aid expired.--The father and mother of this child were notorious in the colony for their loose behaviour; previous to their leaving Sydney they had been wrangling and fighting with each other, and the woman wished every evil might befal her and the infant in her womb (she was six months gone with child) if she went home with her husband--the bodies were found soon after, and Williams buried his wife and child before his own door. This mournful event made not the least impression on this hardened character; for a few days after he had thus buried his wife, he was seen sitting at his door, with a bottle of rum in his hand, and actually drinking one glass himself, and pouring the next over her grave, till it was emptied: saying at every glass "there's your share my old girl," concluding with, "the devil's in it if you won't be quiet now."

Being upon duty, looking out for some of the stragglers, I fell in with one Gray, who had been very notorious for his villainies, and who had eluded the vigilance of the Magistrates at Sydney; I presented my piece and threatned to shoot him if he did not immediately march before me to the settlement, which he did very quietly, and having disposed of him securely for the night, sent him the next morning under a proper escort down to Sydney.

He had formerly been sent to Norfolk Island for several crimes he had committed, and, the term of his sentence being expired, had returned here as a free man; he had hired himself as a servant to one of the New South Wales Corps; one who by great industry and the most rigid economy had scraped up between thirty and forty pounds; but having most indiscreetly made this fellow acquainted with his riches, and also where he kept them, the natural propensity to stealing reigning paramount in this gentleman's constitution, he made no scruple of moving off with the whole sum and several other articles which lay in his way. When upon his trial, he very readily admitted the fact, and on being urged to restore the property, he mentioned a spot where he said he had secured it, but those that were sent not being able to find it, he was conducted to the place himself, when, accidentally meeting the Lieutenant Governor by the way, in order to interest his humanity in his favor, he threw himself on the ground, counterfeiting the most terrible convulsions, but his artifice was too shallow,--he was instantly tied up and punished with 100 lashes. After this he would not make any discovery, and as there was no direct evidence against him, he was sent to the Hospital, and soon after discharged.

Yeariana had now become, as it were, a part of my family, seldom spending a day in a week with her old friends; Batchery could not be persuaded on any account to leave the farm, and as he began to jabber a little English I found him very useful. My domestic concerns were now assuming a very promising aspect, when they were suddenly deranged by an adventure in which Palerino, the brother of Yeariano, was the principal personage.

Palerino had been with me at the farm, and in the afternoon I had persuaded him to take a tiff of weak punch, which I had made to alleviate my thirst, it being a very sultry day;--the beverage pleased him, and he made repeated applications to the jug till he fairly finished its contents. This unusual drink soon operated upon him, causing his eyes to sparkle, and he became quite merry and frolicksome: the punch being made weak, did not produce on him any disagreeable effect.

He took his leave about an hour before sunset, and had proceeded nearly half-way, when he fell in with a party of the tribe of Tugegal, who were wrangling, and appeared ready to go to loggerheads. Palerino recognised among them one of his most intimate friends, and at the same instant saw him knocked down with a club by one of the party;--exhilerated with what he had drank, Palerino flew upon the aggressor like a tyger, and wresting the club from him struck him to the ground, the blow falling on the temple, and being a very violent one, proved his immediate death. The rest of the party not being of kin to the deceased took no part in the fray. They bore off the body on their shoulders, leaving the termination of the affair to be settled by his relations.

Palerino very soon perceived the dangerous situation which his intemperate zeal had hurried him into, and on his return home apprized the family of what had happened.

The very high sense of honour inherent in these people, prevented Palerino from endeavouring to evade the enquiries that were made after him by the friends of the deceased,--he promised to be ready to surrender himself into their hands, and accordingly a day was appointed for retribution.

It is a custom among them that when one kills another of a different tribe, if they are on friendly terms,--whosoever should be the offender--to surrender him up to the party aggrieved; and he is destined to be speared to death, as an expiatory sacrifice to the manes of their murdered friend.

The news of this rencounter reaching the farm by means of Batcherry, plunged Yeariano in the deepest distress; she well knew that her brother's life would be the forfeit of his indiscretion; and, notwithstanding my utmost entreaties, and endeavours to soothe her, she forced herself from my arms, and quitting my habitation, took the road to Paculbenah, the residence of her tribe, with such speed that it was impossible to overtake her.

In a state of the most disagreeable and painful incertitude I remained for about ten days, my business of Peace Officer requiring my constant attendance, I could not leave the district without express permission or upon duty; the disorderly and riotous behaviour of the convicts in general rendering it absolutely necessary to keep a strict and continual watch upon their conduct.

I was relieved from this suspence by Batchery, from whose countenance I conjectured that nothing very terrible had happened, I asked where his sister was, he smiled, and said "you forget poor Palerino--tho he be very well too" then said I "Yeariana is well?" "ees, ees, very well, she be here presently," and before I had time to ask any more questions, a gentle tap made me look round, when my eyes met those of the lovely girl, beaming with love, satisfaction and joy. She made me understand that her brother had been happily extricated from the perilous situation which his late adventure had brought him into.

It seems that the young native in whose defence Palerino had stepped forward, was the favorite Son of the Chief; and was beloved and highly respected by the whole tribe. The evening of the day that Palerino was to expiate his offence with his life, the two tribes collected together, and proceeded to Pannerong (signifying the field of blood) where they spent the night in feasting and dancing; nor did the devoted victim appear as though the next morning was to be the last of his existence, but seemed as unconcerned and conducted himself with as much ease and cheerfulness as any of the company.

A little before sunrise the ceremony began, and forming themselves into a long square, Palerino, attended by two of his own tribe, deliberately and with a firm step walked to the center, where he was met by Warennee, and his father, the chief, who took Palerino by the hand, and told him that as it was a single blow which occasioned the death of Oroodeo, unaccompanied by any other violence, they should consider it as an accident, and that too occasioned by the brutish and ill behaviour of the deceased;--that the custom of his being exposed to the spears of the relations must be complied with, but on account of the circumstances before set forth, it had been agreed that he should be indulged with a shield, when they should see whether he was as skillful in acting on the defensive, as he was bold and powerful in the attack--he then gave him his own shield, and withdrew on one side.

The throwing now began at forty paces distant; the agility and dexterity with which he avoided their aim were loudly extolled by the spectators; when an accident put an end to the contest and relieved Palerino from his dangerous situation;--one of a different tribe being present, was very busy picking up and returning the spears, and being off his guard, was killed on the spot by a random spear--a general shout ensued, and the ceremony was ended, without Palerino receiving a single hurt;--the blood thus accidentally shed was considered as sufficient; altho it was more than probable that whenever his tribe got intelligence of the event, it would occasion a more serious meeting.

Palerino was conducted home, amidst the caresses of both tribes, and the friendship which had for some time subsisted between them was now strongly cemented, by the chief giving him his beautiful daughter, Oteniate, for his wife. The young folks had been no strangers to each other, and were mutually pleased.

The happy winding-up of this tragical business was very gratifying to all the settlers here about; as Palerino was a great favorite, and always ready to oblige them, frequently as a guide, for three or four days together, so that his loss would have been much regretted.

Some settlers having arrived in transports were allotted a tract of land at the upper part of the harbour, and being free people, the spot was christened by the name of Liberty Plains.

Chapter II.

Two Spanish Ships, upon a voyage of discovery, came into the harbour, called the Discovery and the Intrepid, the former wore the broad pendant of a Commodore. They had been three years and a half from Europe, and had ran down the coast of South America, visiting all the Spanish possessions, and precisely ascertaining their boundaries, and situations, whereby they had gained much information.

An officer belonging to them having walked up to Parramatta, I had the honor of dining with him; he was of Irish extraction, and spoke English as his mother tongue; he was a well informed man, and his conversation eagerly listened too. The afternoon was spent with great hilarity, nor did we break up till near midnight, so much were the company charmed with the information, and pleasant manners of this accomplished stranger.

A depredation was discovered to have been made upon the stores, and was carried on in the following manner; two convicts had been employed in issuing the provisions under the storekeeper; they had contrived usually to give an extra allowance to two or three messes, each mess consisting of six people, during the absence of the storekeeper, which often happened while they were serving; when one of each of the mess who were in the league with those who served, took their allowance and hurried off with it;--on the return of the storekeeper the man serving out, call'd the messes over again which had been already served, and they received a second time their allowance, this plot was at last divulged by one of the wives of the party when she was in liquor.

On the examination of the parties it came out that this practice had been pursued for some months, and the different persons concerned being apprehended twere all severely punished by order of the Lieutenant Governor.

A quarrel happening at the hut a of female convict between Abraham Gordon and Richard Sutton; being both very much inflamed with liquor, Sutton was stabbed in the Belly, and otherwise dangerously wounded; Gordon was instantly apprehended; some people were also taken up at Parramatta on suspicion of nightly depredations, also of having killed one of the watchmen belonging to the settlement; the circumstances of which one of them had been overheard relating to a fellow convict; but after much investigation nothing could be brought home to them and they were accordingly discharged.

A soldier who had been sentenced three hundred lashes, on being led out to receive his punishment, attempted to cut his throat, and actually wounded himself pretty deeply under the ear with a knife. The punishment was put off 'till the Evening, when he avowed that he was the person who killed the watchman, and that he would point out the spot where he had secreted the body--This not preventing him from receiving as much of the punishment as he could bear; he afterwards declared that he knew nothing of the murder, and that he only accused himself merely in the hope of deferring his punishment.

Crimes now began to multiply fast upon our hands, On Saturday the 24th. of May, a settler had been drinking at the house of Williams, with Rose Burke, a woman with whom he lived, until they were very much intoxicated, and as they were returning to his farm through the town of Parramatta, a violent quarrel arose between them; when his musquet went off by accident, and shattered the bones of her right arm below the elbow so dreadfully that instant amputation was necessary, which Mr. Arndel the Surgeon being fortunately at home directly performed.

The new grants since the departure of governor Philip amounted to nearly two thousand acres, one half of which lay between Sydney and Parramatta, it being the design of government to establish a range of farms so as to connect those settlements as much as possible, which was a most desirable object to the inhabitants of both.

A dangerous mutiny broke out among the sailors of the Kitty Transport,--the master had frequently complained of the disorderly conduct of his people, several of whom had been punished in consequence; one in particular, Benjamin Williams, had received one hundred lashes.--This man had procured a gallon of rum from one of the convicts, whose term of transportation had expired, and had obtained permission to take his passage home in the Kitty. With this liquor they were carousing, and being noisy in their cups, disturbed the master, who instantly rose and went to the forecastle, where he found them with a candle burning, stuck on the head of an oil cask, and the men in a state nearly bordering upon intoxication: he ordered them to put out the light and go to their hammocks, which they refused; Williams declaring that if he (the master) put it out it should be lit again--the master stepping forward to extinguish it himself, they immediately seized hold of him, and dragging him upon deck actually threw him overboard, before the mate, or any of the rest of the ship's company could come to his assistance. Fortunately he could swim very well, and the mate throwing him a rope over the quarter, he swam to it and got safely on board.

Notwithstanding this daring outrage the captain was disposed to pass it over, and would have inconsiderately put to sea next morning; but when he ordered them to hoist the top-sails, and prepare to get the ship under way, Williams stood forward, and declared that she should not be moved until their complement of hands was on board. The anchor, however, was got up with the assistance of the passengers, and colonists, who had a boat along-side, and she gradually dropped down the harbour.

In the interim the governor being informed of the transactions, ordered a signal to be made for the Kitty to bring to, and immediately went on board, being determined by a striking example, not only to crush the present disorder, but to deter others from committing similar outrages. He ordered Williams and two others of the most refractory to be taken on shore, and replaced them with two convicts of exemplary character, and a seaman, who had been discharged from the Daedalus: tranquillity and order being restored, the ship braced about, and stood out to sea with a fair ind.

The mutineers on their landing were conducted to the parade, where they received, the reward which they richly deserved; Williams two hundred and fifty, and his companions, being less culpable, one hundred and fifty lashes each; after which they were delivered over to the care of an overseer, with strict injunctions that they should be made to earn the provisions which they consumed.

His majesty's birth day was celebrated with the usual festivity--three vollies were fired by the regiment on the parade, and the governor caused twelve of the largest hogs to be slaughtered, and divided among the people in the hospital and the convalescents.

Several attempts had been made to import cattle into this colony, but with very bad success: at this time there had been twelve bulls and upwards of a hundred cows lost on their passage--of all the cattle that were landed, two bulls, twenty cows and two calves, were only living at this period, (June 1793.)--Horses, sheep and hogs were found to stand the rough weather, generally met in the passage from the Cape of Good Hope to this country, much better than the horned cattle.

It is now about three years since the colony experienced a very serious loss: A convict, entrusted with the grazing, by a strange and unaccountable neglect, permitted two bulls and four cows to stray into the woods. He had been strictly enjoined never to lose sight of them; to this order he had paid little attention; he frequently left them and went home to his dinner; till at last on his return to the spot where he had left them, he found that they had quitted it; distracted with fear of the punishment that awaited him, he remained in the woods searching for them, till he was absolutely perishing with hunger, and was found in a most deplorable condition by one of the parties that had been sent out after him.

After a fruitless search for nearly a fortnight, all hopes of finding them were despaired of, and it was conjectured that they had been driven away by the natives: we were afterwards confirmed in this idea, as some of them declared that they had seen them killed, and offered to point out the spot where they had deposited the bones: the place they mentioned being a considerable distance off, the governor declined any farther search. It was very probable that they had been destroyed:--if by chance they had escaped, and were yet living, their numbers must have been considerably increased.

The natives becoming very troublesome, lurking about the different farms, robbing and wounding the convicts whenever they met them without arms;--parties of the military were sent out to drive them from their haunts; yet, notwithstanding, many found means to continue in the towns, and mix with the inhabitants--it was a common thing to fee them coming into the town loaded with firewood, which they had been hired to procure, or bringing water from the tanks; for which services they thought themselves well paid with a worn-out jacket, trowsers, pieces of blanket, or a little bread, of which they were extravagantly fond.

As much inconvenience had been experienced from not having a church, divine service having been hitherto performed in the open air, exposed to the ardent rays of a scorching sun, the Reverend Mr. Johnston, himself, undertook to remove the evil.

Having fixed upon a spot, at the back of the huts, the building was begun under his own inspection. The front was seventy three feet, and the depth about forty; it was constructed with strong posts, entrelaced with wattles, and filled up with plaister; the roof was thatched, not yet being able to afford tiles for so large a building. Great praise was due to the truly christian-like benevolence of our worthy pastor for his personal and unwearied exertions in the erection of this spacious edifice.

The convicts had never yet relaxed in their attendance on Sundays, but had not the conduct of the minister endeared himself to the convicts in general, it would not now have been practicable to enforce a full audience;--the solicitous attention he individually bestowed on the whole community continually crowded his new church.

A plot had lately been discovered which had for its end, the seizing and carrying off one of the long boats--the ringleaders of this business were some soldiers, and their plan was to proceed to Java, a chart of which they had by some means or other procured; had they succeeded they would (to use a homely proverb) have jumped out of the frying pan into the fire; for the Dutch are too jealous of strangers to give them any encouragement, so that in all probability they would have been reduced to the alternative, either of enlisting into their service, a sure and certain method of shortening their days in that premature grave of Europeans, or being kept prisoners till some English ship should touch there to take them off.

Two of the soldiers were immediately put in confinement; and in the night two others absconded into the woods with their arms and all the ammunition they could collect; the two in confinement were brought to a court martial, one of whom was acquitted; but a drummer, named Roberts, for endeavouring to persuade another drummer to be of the party, was sentenced to receive three hundred lashes.

The parties who had been sent after the runaways, by dividing themselves, soon found out their haunt; they were taken without opposition, and escorted back to the settlement, and a few days afterwards they underwent a similar sentence with Roberts.

Some persons had been displaying their ingenuity in the fabricating of counterfeit Dollars, and many were in circulation, two of which among others, I was unlucky enough to get for some stock which I had taken down to Sydney to dispose of. They were ably executed, and notwithstanding a handsome reward was promised to the informer, and a strict search after the manufacturer he remained undiscovered.

About this time a transport from Ireland arrived, with one hundred and fifty convicts of that country, male and female; a party of the New South Wales Corps had embarked with them, and it proved a very salutary precaution; as the spirit of mutiny soon broke out, and they had the hardihood to attempt taking the Ship, but were happily frustrated by the vigilance, spirit, and activity of the master and officers.

Representations having been made to government that the masters of the transports did not take proper care of the health of the convicts, when in their charge, they entered into an agreement to pay the contractors five pounds in addition for every convict that they should land in a healthy state at the settlement. The propriety, and salutary effects of this arrangement, were fully evinced, by the appearance of those lately landed;--each were allowed a hammock and bed to themselves during the passage, and a New suit of clothes to land in;--they unanimously gave testimony to the good treatment they had met with by three cheers to the Captain on going from along side the Ship.

Chapter III.

We now heard of the agitated state of Europe, and of the war having commenced with the French, and that administration had made arrangements for our being supplied with cattle from the East Indies, fearing that in a state of warfare our supplies might be cut off by the enemy; this precaution gave great satisfaction to the settlement at large, for the Bengal Sheep though small, were very productive, breeding twice in the year, and mostly bringing two lambs at a time. An instance of the remarkable fecundity of a goat happened in the house of one of the superintendants at Sydney, she produced five kids, all of which died from a blow she received while in kid: seven months afterwards she gave birth to four, all of which lived; she was the most beautiful animal I ever saw.

A ship being about to sail for England, seven persons, whose term of transportation had expired, were permitted to embark themselves;--Passages to Europe from hence were procured with the greatest facility (little more being required than permission to receive them, and the finding their provisions,) yet it was frequently the case that convicts secreted themselves on board without leave, as was the case in this ship; (the Sugar Cane) for the day she sailed two were sent back who had not obtained their certificate for which they were punished with fifty lashes each.

The New South Wales Corps was now augmented;--thirty recruits, who had been selected from among the convicts, bearing good Characters, and having been formerly soldiers, were permitted to enlist; they behaved as well as any of the Corps; one of them only excepted, who was for misbehaviour afterwards discharged, and reduced to his former situation. A reinforcement of twenty three more was added, which made up the full complement of convicts that was intended to be admitted into the Corps. The condition of enlisting was that of their serving in the regiment till regularly discharged.

Many irregularities and robberies being frequently committed in and about Parramatta, my post as Peace Officer, became very troublesome; being obliged to be ever on the watch to suppress disorders, and apprehend all suspicious and straggling persons who could not render a good account of themselves.--On the 15th. of October four people broke into the house of John Randall, one of the settlers, within a hundred paces from my house, and nearly murdered two men who lived with him.--The hands and faces of these plunderers were blackened to avoid detection, and they observed the strictest silence while they were in the hut, that their voices might not betray them, they were prevented from robbing the premises by the spirited resistance they met with. The Irish Convicts, who had taken to the woods were soon apprehended; they confessed that they had formed a plan to rob the mill house, the governor's and several others, and that they were to be visited from time to time in their concealment, by their associates in the town, who were to supply them with provisions, and such information as was necessary for their safety, they also acknowledged that the attack on Randal's house was committed by them and their associates.

Soon after this the house of Mr Atkins, notwithstanding the sharpest look out, was broke open, and plundered of a large quantity of provisions; and a quarter cask of wine was taken from the store, but left in the garden on their being disturbed; they however carried off a large booty.

A severe storm of rain and thunder happened on Saturday the 26th. of October 1793, two Convicts, Dennis Reardon, and William Meredith, who were employed in cutting wood just without the town, ran to a tree for shelter in the beginning of the storm, where they were found next morning lying dead, with a dog that had followed them. There was little doubt but the shelter which they had sought had proved their destruction, and that they had been struck dead by the lightning, as the flashes were observed to have been very vivid, and hovering over the tree where they were found; the pupils of their eyes appeared much injured, and their tongues were forced out between their teeth; their faces were discoloured, as were also several parts of their bodies; the tree was stripped of its bark from top to bottom, and some of its branches were torn off. This was the first accident of the kind that had occurred in the colony, though lightning more ardent and alarming had often appeared, and storms of a much longer duration.

Williams the settler, whom I before have had occasion to mention, wearied of being in a state of independence, sold his farm with the house crop and stock, for a little less than £100. to an officer whose ground was contiguous; another settler, anxious to return to England, followed his example; in consequence they had to seek employment from others till an opportunity occurred of their getting a passage home.

A convict of the name of Crow fell in my way as I was out on the patrol, against whom there were several charges; I accordingly apprehended him, and saw him safely lodged in the military guard house at Paramatta, from which, however, he found means to escape, and, rambling down to Sydney Cove, swam off to a transport in the harbour, the master of which immediately took him on shore--he received a slight punishment and was put in the black-hole at Sydney, out of which he also effected his liberation, by untiling a part of the roof of his prison, and was not heard of for some time; when he again fell in my way, between Parramatta and Toongabbe, where he had been committing fresh depredations, having actually broken open two houses, considerable property from which was now found upon him.

The frequent commission of capital offences had rendered it necessary to inflict punishments more likely to prevent the perpetration of crimes than a mere flogging;--Crow was therefore delivered over to the civil power, and ordered to be tried by the criminal court of judicature.--He was accordingly tried on the second of December, and being clearly convicted, sentence of death was passed upon him--two others were tried with him, but they were acquitted, for want of sufficient evidence, although the whole court were fully assured of their guilt:

Crow was ordered for immediate execution, but petitioning for a respite it was granted him till the tenth, when he justly forfeited his life, as an atonement for the depredations he had committed on society. Just before he suffered he had nearly effected his escape a third time--with much labour and ingenuity he had displaced some bricks from the wall, covering the interstices so neatly that they were scarcely perceptible: being discovered, by the vigilant eye of the centinel, he next attempted the necessary, but not succeeding there, his spirits failed him, and he exhibited more weakness and dismay at the place of execution than was expected from such a determined character.

Chapter IV.

Many Officers now began to avail themselves of the permission which had been granted them of cultivating land; several of them fixed at Parramatta and its neighbourhood, whereby I gained a most valuable acquisition in the friendship and acquaintance of several gentlemen, who passing over the shade of my past life, deigned to make me their companion, and I flatter myself my future conduct shall never put them to the blush for their condescendsion.

They commenced their occupation of farmers in the highest spirits--Tools and implements for husbandry were furnished by Government, and they were allowed the labour of ten convicts each, by which they made great progress; also by the hire of extra hands on those days that they were not employed for the public; and as they were not restrained from paying them in liquors, they easily obtained as many Gangs as they could employ.

The passion for liquor still predominated over every other consideration, there being nothing which they would not risk to obtain it: and while spirits were to be had, they would take no other article in pay for their labour, and which were now sold so high as Six Shillings a bottle--A Settler near Parramatta having procured a small still from England, obtained a deleterious and mischievous spirit from his Wheat, which he found more profitable than carrying it to the public store, and selling it for ten Shillings per bushell. From one bushell of wheat he extracted nearly five quarts of spirits, which he sold, or paid for labour, at the rate of five and six shillings a bottle: hence proceeded the shocking immorality now visible in the convicts, hence the frequent robberies, and disorders in the settlements, and their total disregard to all decency and neglect of Divine worship--formerly the worthy Pastor had an audience of two or three hundred; but now, on Christmas day, he preached to about thirty persons, and the evening produced a watch house full of prisoners; the greater part in a state of intoxication.

Mr. Mc, Donald, a settler at the field of Mars--a settlement so called from its being first occupied by men discharged from the marines--made a different use of the produce of his Farm. Having a mill he ground and dressed his wheat, which he sold to a baker at Sydney for four pence the pound; one bushell of wheat producing forty four pounds of flour--He also killed a weather Sheep, produced from some that had been given him by Governor Philip, and sold it at two Shillings per pound, the quarters weighing about fifteen pounds. Sydney town had considerably increased since the departure of Governor Philip, not less than one hundred and sixty huts and five barracks having been added; some of the huts were large and commodious, and to each of them fifteen hundred bricks were allowed for a chimney and floor, each hut was twenty six feet in front, and fourteen in width, and were divided into apartments for ten convicts, a proportionate spot of garden-ground was reserved for each building.

About Christmas a large party of the natives attacked some settlers who were returning from Parramatta to Toongabbe, and took from them the provisions which they had just received from the store--They instantly made off into the woods; and though they were immediately pursued we could not overtake them. They were of the hunter or woodman's tribe, who were seldom among us, and consequently very little known. The natives who lived about Sydney placed the utmost confidence in us, choosing a cleared spot near the town for the performance of their rites and ceremonies, and for three successive evenings the town had been amused with one of their spectacles which might very properly be termed a tragic comedy; for, though some blood was shed, no lives were lost. It is the custom as before observed with respect to Palerino, that the person who was the cause of another's death, was compelled to meet the relations of the deceased, who were to avenge the death by throwing spears and drawing blood for blood.--A native of the tribe of Cammerray, a very fine fellow named Carradah, who had stabbed another in the night, but not mortally, was obliged to make the amende honourable, by standing two evenings exposed to the spearing of the relations of the wounded man. He was indulged with a bark shield, and defended himself with great skill and resolution, and the first day ended without his receiving a single wound. But on the next evening, after having exhausted the patience of his opponents, and remaining unhurt, the wounded man walked up very composedly to Carradah, who suffered him to pin his arm to his side with his spear, without the least resistance; prevented, very probably, by the threatning and uplifted spears of the other natives, who could easily have destroyed him, by throwing at him in different directions. Carradah stood for some time after this, defending himself, although wounded in the arm which held the shield, until his adversaries had not a spear left, and they retired to gather up the fragments of the broken spears. The business was resumed when they had repaired their weapons, it then appeared a battle Royal, men, women, and children mingled in it, in the course of which many severe wounds were given and received ere night ended the warfare. We never could account for this extraordinary contest; for the utmost cordiality and friendship subsisted between the different parties who fought each other with all the fury of the most implacable enemies, and those worsted in the conflict, spoke of their opponents as brave men, and their friends.

The wounds of the combatants were soon healed, and it was understood that Carradah had yet another trial to sustain from some of the natives who had been prevented by absence from joining in the ceremonies of that evening, Carradah was very intimate in the town, and had exchanged names with Mr. Ball, who commanded the Supply, he went after by that name which the natives pronounced Midjer Bool.

Chapter V.

Another barrack was now building at Sydney, but for want of the tiles was not finished; two mill-wrights had also got up the frames and roofs of two mill-houses, and while they were waiting for the tiles endeavoured to forward the wood-work; the great want of tiles proceeded from there being only one person who understood the moulding them, and he never could burn more than five thousand in a week, being obliged to burn a great number of bricks in the same kilns. It required near Seventy thousand bricks to complete the building of one barrack, and twenty thousand tiles to cover it in--to furnish bricks for these barracks and other buildings, three gangs were constantly at work, which comprised three overseers and eighty convicts--The distance from the brick fields to the barracks was about three quarters of a mile, three brick carts were employed conveying these materials, each drawn by twelve men, under the direction of an overseer--seven hundred tiles, or three hundred and fifty bricks were a load; and every cart was expected to make five turns in the day. The bringing in of the timber was also a most laborious work; There were four timber carriages employed, each drawn by twenty four men; every carriage was attended by two fellers, and an overseer[?], making in the whole two hundred and twenty eight men, exclusive of sawyers, carpenters, smiths, painters, glaziers, and stone masons; the Provisioning and Clothing all these people must be very considerable, and will be found to amount to an enormous sum when the expences of the public works erected in this colony come to be calculated.

On the 5th, of January 1794. A most atrocious murder was committed on the body of John Lewis, an elderly man, who was employed to graze the cattle of Parramatta. The beasts having lost their conductor, remained all night in the woods; they were found next morning, but no tidings of Lewis could be got, which caused it to be apprehended that some accident had happened him. It was some days before his body was found, and was at last pointed out by the snorting and uneasiness of the cattle when they came to a particular spot; having been drove out on purpose by way of experiment. It was laying in a ravine, into which it had been thrown by the murderers, who had covered it with logs, branches of trees and grass. Some native dogs allured by the scent of blood had already been mangling the carcase, which added to the horrible spectacle it exhibited.

This unfortunate man had imprudently boasted of being worth a sum of money, and that he always carried it about him, sewed up in his clothes, in case his hut should be robbed during his absence. By the number of wounds he had received, he must have defended himself stoutly, and was certainly overpowered by numbers, being a stout muscular man;--to discover, if possible, the murderers, several people of bad characters were apprehended and examined, but nothing transpired that could attach to any of them, and the enquiry dropped, with an expectation that the perpetrators would sooner or later be brought to punishment, and that some riot or disagreement among themselves would furnish a clue, that would infallibly lead to detection.

The pernicious vice of gaming which had rapidly obtained in the settlement, and which was carried on to such excess among the convicts that many had been known, after losing their provisions, money, and spare cloathing, to bet, and lose the very clothes from their backs, exhibiting themselves as naked, and as indifferent about it, as the natives of the country.--Money was their principal object; for with it they could purchase spirits, which they greedily coveted. They have frequently been seen playing at their favourite games of Cribbage and All Fours, for ten dollars a game, and those who were ignorant of those games would be content to toss up for dollars, instead of halfpence. Their meetings were scenes of quarrelling swearing, and every wickedness that might be expected by a description of people totally destitute of the least particle of shame; but glorying in their depravity. To this dreadful vice in a great measure may be attributed most of the crimes that existed in the colony.

It was found that the settlers, notwithstanding the plentiful crops which they generally gathered, gave no assistance to government, by sending it into store, for which (as before observed) they were allowed Ten Shillings per Bushel, a very small quantity had been sent in, and totally inadequate to their wants or expectation. They seemed ungratefully to prefer any other mode, than what in justice or gratitude they ought to have pursued; some by clandestinely brewing and distilling it, others by paying debts contracted by gambling, as even the farms themselves, were some times staked, and lost at a game of Hazard.

In this month (January) another division of settlers was added--Williams and Rouse having squandered away the money for which they had sold their farms, were permitted, with some others, to settle on the banks of the Hawksbury, about 24 Miles from Parramatta. They pitched upon a spot desirably situated with respect to water, and where it did not require much labour to clear it;--they began with great alacrity and spirit; and formed very sanguine hopes of success. At the end of the month they had cleared several acres, and were in great forwardness with their huts, nor were they in the least interrupted by the natives--not so in this neighbourhood, where it might have been supposed that they would have expected such resistance as they would not have chose to encounter. However, be that as it may, several settlers about Parramatta had been attacked by armed parties, and robbed of their clothing and provisions.

Many reports of this kind had been brought into the town, perhaps some of them might have been fabricated, to conceal the effects of their gambling--Notwithstanding it was clearly apparent that these people were ever on the watch, and it was observed that as the corn ripened they constantly approached nearer the farms and the public grounds, for the purpose of depredation.

William Crozier Cook, having rendered himself obnoxious to the law, had absconded into the woods, where not being able to grind the wheat he had stolen from the store he ate it unground, which upon drinking a quantity of water fermented in his bowels, and caused a mortification, and notwithstanding, (on his being obliged from the excessive torments he endured to crawl into the town) the most efficacious medicines were administred he soon after expired.

In the beginning of February two Watches which had been missing were discovered, and taken down to Sydney. Upon investigation it appeared they had been stolen by John Bevan, who at the time had broken out of the Prison Hut of Toongabba, a settlement near Parramatta, and getting down to Sydney committed the theft in conjunction with Sutton, who had been before tried for a similar offence; he had returned with the spoil to his hut, before he had been missed by any of the watchmen.--Playing at cards some time afterwards with other convicts, he exchanged the watches for a Nankeen jacket and trowsers.--From this they went from one to the other till at length they were found in the possession of one Batty, in the thatch of whose house they were discovered, together with ten dollars, which were supposed to be part of the money of a man who had been robbed in the hospital, with whom Bevan had been intimate, and had won from him an hundred weight of flour which he had almost starved himself to hoard up--he also inveigled him out of the secret of his having money, and all the particulars that were necessary to his design of stealing it.

This information was gained from the people through whose hands the watches had passed; but it being unsupported by any corroborating evidence, the court, though thoroughly convinced of his guilt, was under the necessity of giving him an acquital--Batty and another man, Normanton, whose guilt was sufficiently proved, received each a severe punishment.

Chapter VI.

In the foregoing part I promised to transmit an account of the rise and progress of the Colony at Norfolk Island, but have hitherto been prevented, by the delay occasioned from Mr. Wentworth being so fully occupied that he had not leisure to write me the particulars at once, however, from our correspondence I hope I shall be able to collect a Narrative which I presume will not be uninteresting to the reader.

Governor Philip, previous to his leaving England, had received orders to establish a Colony at Norfolk Island as soon as possible after his arrival in New-South Wales; and to shew that no time was lost, he dispatched Lieutenant King, of the Sirius, in the Supply, tender, the middle of February, (not more than a month after his arrival in the country) investing him with the Offices of Superintendant and commandant of the Settlement. Mr. King, previous to his departure for his little government, was sworn in as a justice of the peace, which enabled him to punish such petty offences as might be committed among his people--capital crimes being reserved for the cognizance of the criminal court of judicature, established at Sydney.

Lieutenant King took with him one Surgeon, one Petty officer, (Mr. Cunningham) two privates, two persons who pretended to have some knowledge of flax-dressing, nine male, and six female convicts, with provisions for six months.

Norfolk Island is situated in 29 degrees South Lattitude, and 168 degrees East Longitude, and was settled with a view to the cultivation of the Flax-Plant, which at the time it was discovered by Captain Cook, was found in great abundance, and from specimens taken to England of the New Zealand Flax, which is of the same kind as that at Norfolk Island, it was hoped that the mother-country might derive great advantage from its cultivation.

The Supply arrived at the Island on the 29th. of February, 1788, but it was five days before any landing could be effected, occasioned by a surf breaking violently over a reef of rocks, which crossed the principal bay. Their patience was nearly exhausted, and it was almost determined to return; judging that a spot so difficult of access was not the most desirable for a new Settlement; when upon standing in a little nearer the shore a small opening was perceptible in the reef, wide enough to admit a boat, through which he and his people landed with all their provisions and stores in perfect safety.

When landed, they found themselves in an impenetrable wilderness, and could not discover a clear spot, sufficient to pitch a tent, so that all hands were immediately set to work in order to clear the ground for the New Settlement, which Mr. King named Sydney-Bay, he had also become sponsor to two small islands in the vicinity, one of which he named Philip, after the Governor, and the other Nepean, in compliment to the present Secretary to the Admiralty.

In the month of August a transport arrived from Port Jackson, having on board a midshipman and two seaman of the Sirius, a serjeant, corporal and a party of marines, also some free settlers with their families. The utmost regularity and industry were observed throughout the settlement for a whole year: when the following plan of an insurrection among the convicts was discovered--They were to commence their operations by the seizure of Mr. King, which was intended to be effected on the first Saturday after the arrival of any ship in the Bay, except the Sirius. Saturday was the day pitched upon, it being generally, the custom of Mr. King on that day to visit a farm he had established a small distance from the settlement. He was accordingly to be surprised and secured in his way to the farm. A message was then to be sent, in his name, to Mr. Jameison, the surgeon, to come immediately to the farm, when he was to be secured directly on his entering the woods;--the serjeant and party were to be treated in the same manner. These being properly taken care of, a signal was to be made to the vessel in the Bay, to send her boat on shore, the crew of which were to be made prisoners on their landing; when two or three of the revolters were to go off in a boat belonging to the Island, and inform the commanding officer that the ship's boat had been stove on the beach, and that the commandant requested that another might be sent on shore; this also was to be captured, and then the ship was to be boarded and taken, with which they were to proceed to Otaheite. We must do them the justice to acknowledge that they meant to leave some provisions for the commandant and his officers--This was their scheme, not one difficulty in the execution whereof had ever occurred to their imagination, and they took it for granted that all was to succeed as easily as they had planned it, and had it not happened to be revealed by a female convict, to Mr. King's gardener, with whom she cohabited, there is no doubt but that this inconsistent plan would have been put in execution. Upon the discovery of their villainous intentions every possible precaution was taken to defeat them. The first step was to clear the ground round the settlement to such a distance, that the woods should not conceal any preparations for a future attempt.

On the 26th. of February they were visited by a hurricane in which several Pine Trees from one hundred and eighty, to two hundred feet, in length, and from twenty to thirty in the girt, were blown down; and by noon the gale increased to such violence that Pines and Oaks were borne down by the fury of the tempest;

which tearing up trees and rocks with them, left chasms of eight and ten feet deep in the earth: those trees that were not torn up by the roots bent till they nearly swept the ground with their tops: a large Oak was blown on the granary, which crushed to pieces, with a number of casks of flour--and nothing but horror and desolation presented itself.

By the activity of the free people and officers the flour, Indian corn, and stores were collected and removed to the commandant's house--a greater number of trees were blown down than could have been felled by fifty men in a month's labour. In the progress of the storm, the whole of the bay and great part of the settlement was covered with water, and the gardens, public and private were totally destroyed. The island had lately received an increase of inhabitants so that at this time they mustered sixteen free people; fifty one male, and twenty three female convicts with four children, who were all in exceeding good health; a certain sign of the goodness of the climate.--For the defence of the Island, the free people formed a Militia, and a guard was mounted every night. The colony still increasing in numbers, it was thought necessary that they should have an additional military Force, accordingly in the month of June, Lieut. Cresswell of the Marines, and fourteen privates arrived from New South Wales.

The greatest assiduity had been used in repairing the ravages of the hurricane, and by the month of August the country not only assumed its former cheerful appearance, but twenty acres of ground had been cleared and sown on the public account--a store-house was now erected capable of containing a large quantity of stores, and a road cut across the Island to Cascade Bay.

The pine trees which were expected to have been a most valuable acquisition for malts and yards, of large ships, were found wholly unfit for the purpose; and no use could be yet made of the flax, owing to the ignorance of the people who had come out as professed flax dressers. However the affairs of the colonists were in the most thriving state, and the harvest had returned more than twenty fold, though they had experienced much dry weather. After the harvest all the spare hands were employed in palisadoing a piece of ground two hundred feet, by one hundred and fifty, encircling the house of the commandant, the public stores, and a military barrack.--This precaution was very highly necessary to guard against a surprize, should any further attempts be made by the villainous and disaffected, many of which description were now on the island.

In the beginning of the year 1790, governor Philip became uneasy at the non-arrival of supplies from England, as the provisions in store, at half-allowance to each man in the colony, would not hold out above four months. They had on their landing a sufficient stock for two years; that time was now elapsed, and had it not been for the great care and economy of the governor, the whole colony must have perished with hunger.

Towards the end of February, no vessels arriving, his excellency judged it absolutely necessary to divide the settlement: he accordingly ordered captain Hunter to prepare the Sirius for sea, and to take on board a number of marines and convicts, and proceed with them to Norfolk Island where there were many resources, which they had not at port Jackson.

The Sirius was soon ready, and on the 6th. of March the weighed anchor, having on board Major Ross, the Lieutenant Governor, one company of marines and officers, and one hundred and eighty six convicts, with a proportion of the remaining provisions, and other stores--The Supply tender, commanded by Lieutenant Ball also took a company of marines, and twenty convicts.

After a week's sail, they arrived at Norfolk Island, and sailing nearly round it, they at last found a spot on which the captain judged that he should be able to land his passengers in safety, the Island being almost entirely begirt with a shoal, or reef of sunken rocks, which caused a heavy surf on the least fresh of wind. The debarkation took place on a rock which projects some distance into the sea, and continued for two days; no sooner had the last boat load landed, than the wind shifted, and set right on the shore; as it began to blow very strong, the ship was obliged to stand out to sea, leaving nearly three hundred people on shore without a possibility of landing any of the provisions or stores. This circumstance alarmed the new settlers, and the more so, as the weather grew so hazey that they soon lost sight of the ship; however, the next morning the Supply came to an anchor in the bay, but the greater part of the provisions and stores being in the Sirius, their apprehensions on her score were increased. In this state of uncertainty they remained for four days, when to their great satisfaction at day break on the 20th. of March they perceived her working into the bay. She soon after brought too, hoisted out the boats which were loaded with provisions and dispatched on shore.

The ship falling very fast to leeward, captain Hunter thought it expedient to make sail, but the reef of sunken rocks extending farther than was imagined, which was now visible; as the sea began to rise the surf broke over them a considerable way out, so that it was not possible for the Sirius to weather it; upon which when they were sufficiently near they attempted to tack, but missed stays and fell off again; they were now obliged to wear her round in as small a space as possible, which was done, and they got under the same sail as before. The ship continuing to fall to leeward, shoaling her water, and being baulked a second time in her attempt to tack, her anchor was let go, but before the cable brought her up, she struck upon the reef; in a few minutes after she bulged, and the water flowed into the hold.

The masts were now cut away in order to lighten her, so that there might be a chance of her swinging over the reef in-shore, whereby the lives of those on board might be saved, which was effected in the course of the day, by means of a hawser, which was floated to the shore by a cask, and made fast to a tree.

Chapter VII.

The preservation of the stores and provisions was their next concern, and as the sea continued turbulent and the weather tempestuous their former fears of starving returned; there being now upon that small island (five miles in length, and three in breadth) no fewer than five hundred souls upon half-allowance of provisions, and that for a very short time, as the chief part was still in the most perilous state.--The severe weather subsiding, they had several very fine days, during which all hands were employed in getting out the provisions and stores. By great exertions, from twenty to thirty casks of provisions were brought from the wreck every day, with various other articles of public and private property; such things as would swim were thrown into the sea to take their chance of being wasted on shore by the surf, and guards were placed on the beach to prevent their being stolen by the convicts: and every thing that was washed a-shore was placed under the charge of the centinels until claimed by the proprietor.

Two of the convicts offered their services to bring on shore what live hogs they could save, but unfortunately they could not withstand the temptation of the spirit-room, in proceeding to which, they set the ship on fire in two places, which being perceived from the shore, a young man named Ascott, a convict, gallantly plunged into the surf, gained the wreck, extinguished the fire and forced the wretches out of the ship.

Before the ship could be cleared, the weather became unfavorable, and the high surf rendered it unsafe for any person to go on board--'till at length a very heavy sea raised her bodily, and shifted her berth a cable's length nearer in-shore, so that it was much easier and safer to send on board, and the greater part of her cargo was safely landed: before we entirely gave her up, we landed even the guns, and all her ordnance stores.

The Lieutenant Governor now called a council of all the naval and military officers, when it was determined that martial law should be proclaimed--that all private stock, poultry excepted, should be considered as the property of the state--that justice should be administered by a court martial, to be composed of seven officers, five of whom were to concur in a sentence of death; and that there should be two keys upon the door of the public store, whereof one was to be in the keeping of a person appointed by Captain Hunter, in behalf of the seamen, the other by a person in behalf of the military. The day following the troops, seamen, and convicts, being assembled, these resolutions were publickly read, and the whole confirmed their engagement of abiding by them, by passing under his Majesty's Flag, which was displayed on a convenient spot, and every person passed under it, bowing as they passed (which they were given to understand signified their assent) this ceremony was performed with proper solemnity and great cheerfulness;--Hitherto every criminal, amenable to trial was to be sent to Port Jackson, with all the necessary evidence, and there tried, which had been attended with great inconveniences. Mr. King, was dispatched in the Supply to Port Jackson with news of the loss of the Sirius, and to entreat that immediate relief might be sent, as the provisions were so very scanty, that the following short weekly allowance was obliged to be resorted to; viz. three pounds of flour, one pound and a half of beef, or one pound of pork, and one pound of rice.

Observing great quantities of birds hovering over a hill which had been christened Mount Pitt, it was conjectured that they might draw some support from thence; accordingly some persons were sent to examine it--They found it perforated like a rabbit-warren, and full of nests; towards the evening such flocks came in from the sea that their numbers were incredible; the people made small fires which attracting their attention they dropped on the ground, and they killed as many as they pleased. When they are upon the ground they cannot raise themselves, owing to the length of their wings, and until they gain an eminence they cannot take to flight:--for this purpose nature has provided them with a sharp spur and a strong hawk's bill, with this assistance they have been seen to climb up a crooked tree sufficiently high to throw themselves on the wing--they are about the size of a pidgeon, web-footed and of a dun colour; they lay but a single egg, but that is full as large as a duck's--the flesh is like that of a puffin, rather fishy; and although they killed between two and three thousand every night they could perceive no diminution of their numbers.

More than six months passed ere any succours arrived from Port Jackson, and the people in general were very much reduced in bodily strength for want of food; when two ships arrived with provisions and a fresh reinforcement of convicts--these supplies were extremely providential, as their greatest resource, Mount Pitt, began to fail in the quantity of birds, and the fishing had entirely ceased.

It was at this time that Mr. Wentworth arrived, and was particularly noticed by Major Ross, who on account of his abilities and reputation immediately appointed him as a superintending surgeon of the Island.

During the residence of Captain Hunter and the crew of the Sirius, he had employed them in blowing up some rocks which obstructed the passage through the reef; their efforts had been attended with great success; correct Surveys had also been made by Lieutenant Bradley, so that a landing was now effected in any weather. The Lieutenant Governor had caused near two hundred acres of land to be cleared, having had great success in the first crops of Maize and Wheat--Two pieces of coarse canvass were manufactured and sent as a specimen to Governor Philip.

Martial law being discontinued, some prisoners for capital offences were sent to New South Wales to be tried, but for want of sufficient evidence they were acquitted--much inconvenience was experienced from this mode--as all the witnesses were obliged to be embarked to attend the trial.--In this case the prosecutor was a settler, and being obliged to leave his farm for the time, his business of course was suspended 'till his return, and his whole concern went to ruin--one of the witnesses also was nearly in the same perdicament. But as the courts here will always be the superior courts, it will not be easily remedied.

Captain Hunter, his officers and men took their passage to Port Jackson, after sharing the fatigues and anxieties of the settlers for the space of eleven months, leaving the Island in a comparative state of plenty.

Soon after captain King, now promoted to the rank of a master and commander; also appointed Lieutenant Governor of the settlement, arrived with his family in the Atlantic transport, and relieved Major Ross, who returned to New South Wales, with his detatchment, on board the Queen.

The frequent visitations to Mount Pitt had greatly thinned the numbers of the birds; more owing to the thoughtless wantonness of the convicts than the quantity killed; for they not only destroyed bird, its young and the egg, but the hole in which it burrowed, and from which they had the most positive orders to refrain; as nothing was more likely to make them forsake the Island.

The governor having discovered that the Island abounded in lime--stones, built a handsome and convenient house for himself, with store houses, Barracks for the soldiery, and other public buildings: he also persevered with respect to the flax-plant, and agreed with the master of a transport to procure him two of the natives of New Zealand, who made good canvas from it in their country; for which service he was to give him one hundred pounds. Two of them were accordingly prevailed on to venture to Norfolk Island, where they resided near a twelvemonth; and having given such instructions as enabled the colonists to manufacture it tolerably well, began to evince a hankering after their own country; the governor therefore was resolved by the first opportunity to gratify their wishes; and that he might be sure that they did not experience any neglect, or ill usage, determined to accompany them himself--He accordingly embarked on board the Britannia, and in a few days restored them to their native country, and their friends.

A jealousy had subsisted for some time between the Soldiery, the free men, and others of the Settlers; frequent sparring and acts of violence had taken place, till at length on the 18th. of January 1794, it broke out in an open warfare, in a place which the governor had permitted the convicts to perform plays, after their working hours. He being present immediately ordered one of the soldiers to be put under an arrest. As soon as the play was finished, the rest of the soldiers in a body repaired to their own commanding officer; and boldly demanded the release of their comrade. On his refusing their request, they signified that they would release him themselves; upon which the officer spiritedly remonstrated with them, and they dispersed. They made no movement towards putting their threats in execution, nevertheless when their conduct was reported to the governor, he convened all the officers together, and laid before them what he had heard; also an account of a determination among the soldiers to release from the halberts any of their comrades, who should be ordered punishment for any injury or offence done to a settler: all of which had been ratified with an oath.--He then pointed out the necessity of punishing the delinquents, which was effected in the following manner.

On the next day the detatchment was sent from their quarters in parties upon different duties, unarmed, when the marines, and settlers who were of the late militia took their arms. On their return, twenty of them were selected as ringleaders, ten of whom were sent to Port Jackson in irons to be tried for mutiny, the other ten received punishment on the island; others were confined for a short time, when the rest returning cheerfully to their duty the affair blew over, and things went on as tranquilly as before.

All remembrance of former scarcity began now to be done away, and upwards of fifty thousand bushels of maize, might have been sent to Port Jackson, had the Lieutenant Governor though proper to fall in with the proposals of Mr. King--His harvests had been extremely productive, and he had purchased from the settlers the surplus of their first-crops;--bills for the amount of which he drew upon government in favour of the respective owners;--but as they required to be approved by the Lieutenant Governor, they were sent to Port Jackson for that purpose:--There being at this juncture a tolerable supply of grain in the settlement, the Lieutenant Governor did not think it prudent to put the crown to so great an expence (nearly four thousand pounds sterling) therefore declined accepting the Bills.

Mr. King had been fully warranted in this procedure not only by the idea that the corn would be acceptable, but that it was one of the express conditions on which the settlers had received their respective allotments, under the regulations of Governor Philip; which was, that the overplus grain and stock should be purchased from them at a fair market price; this circumstance gave great discontent among the settlers, many of whom gave up their farms, and went to Port Jackson.

The ground now cleared, comprised near six thousand acres, about one half of the Island, and the greater part was in high cultivation in 1794 and 1795, and produced upwards of forty thousand bushels of grain; but from the impolitic check given to private industry as before mentioned, the quantity gradually decreased to nearly one half--the ground thus neglected became over-run with strong thick weeds, which gave harbour to the numerous rats with which the island abounds, besides the injury done to the soil, which was much to be lamented; however, it is to be hoped that--as through the humane interference of governor Hunter the corn bills are now paid, and a notification that all the surplus grain would be purchased in future by government--the industrious disposition of the settlers will again revive.

The inhabitants on the island are divided into six classes, First, the Civil and the Military--second, Settlers by grant, or lease, Freeman hired, and Convicts taken off the stores by officers; the third class consists of Convicts allowed to officers as servants and overseers. Artificers, Watchmen. Those employed in husbandry for the public, and other incidental work, compose the fourth class. The fifth and sixth comprize the women and children.

There were two schools;--one for young children who were instructed by a very decent woman;--the other kept by a man, who taught reading, writing and arithmetic, for which he was well qualified, and was very attentive: another institution was added for the reception of orphans. It was unfortunate that these as well as the other children were destitute of every article of cloathing, except such as the store afforded, which was not at all calculated for them in that warm climate. In order to support these institutions a subscription was raised among the officers, and fines were imposed in lieu of other punishments for breaches of the peace & c. all of which were applied to that purpose.

The state of the flax-manufactory is not such as to boast of, being in great want of tools; they have but one loom, and the only cloth they at present make is a canvas something finer than No. 7--which is equally strong and durable with that made of European flax.

Before the arrival of the two New Zealanders no progress had been made in this manufacture, and it was with great difficulty they could be persuaded to give any information respecting it, and indeed as the work is generally performed in New Zealand by the women, they were not competent to give the fullest instruction: Sufficient however was obtained to proceed thus far, and since their departure such women as could be spared from other work, about twelve in number, had been employed in preparing the flax, and a flax-dresser, weaver, and three assistants, in manufacturing it into Canvas, Rope & c.

The convicts are employed according to their respective trades, and work from day-light till eight o'clock,--from nine till noon, and from two in the afternoon till sun-set. On Fridays and Saturdays they are allowed to work for themselves, or whoever chuses to hire them; they are also indulged by government with the loan of tools and materials. Husbandmen and Labourers work from day light 'till one o'clock, and have the rest of the day to themselves, which is found to be more eligible than letting them break off to their meals.

The price of labour for a convict is from five to six pounds per annum--A Freeman, clothed and victualled, twelve pounds.--A day's--work for a labourer is three shillings, allowing him provisions, otherwise five--Clearing an acre of wood, two pounds, an acre of weeds, thirty shillings--Threshing of Wheat, twenty pence the bushel--other work is done in proportion--the mode of payment for which, is according to the circumstances of the employer; in stock, grain, European Articles, and sometimes, though very rarely, in cash,--Provisions at the time Mr. Wentworth left the island were very reasonable; Fresh Pork, six pence a pound; Pickled Pork, eight pence; Wheat from seven to ten shillings a bushel; Potatoes three shillings the hundred weight; Fowls from sixpence to a shilling; Ducks from ten pence to fifteen pence; Turkeys, seven shillings and sixpence; Geese, ten shillings; She Goats, eight pounds each; Goats flesh, eighteen pence per pound; these last articles were dear, owing to the scarcity; but on the whole not more than one third of the price they bore here. European commodities were nearly at the same price. The inhabitants amounted to nearly one thousand, about six hundred men, and the remainder women and children: the births for these last five years have been one hundred and ninety six, and the deaths one hundred and forty two, forty of which were under two years of age. At this time plenty reigned throughout the island, every barn was full and several thousand pounds of fresh pork had been cured, and fifty tons of salt provisions in store; so that it may now be stated that the colony is fully and completely established. Governor King having by unremitting exertions brought his little colony to this degree of perfection; now turned his thoughts towards England, as the only means of restoring his health, which had been greatly impaired; and on the 23rd. of October, 1796, he embarked with his family on board the Britannia Transport for England; Mr Wentworth had arrived here in the beginning of the year, having received an appointment in this colony.

Chapter VIII.

In the commencement of the year 1794 the colony was prodigiously alarmed on account of the great scarcity of provisions--The public store had never been in such a reduced state; a reduction of two pounds of wheat per week, had taken place, and only one serving of salt provisions left, which was only half a week's-allowance; after that period, bread and water would be the only resource of the greater part of the inhabitants; but fortunately on Saturday the 8th. of March, when the doors of the store had been finally closed, and the convicts had received their last ration of salt meat, the signal for a sail was made--and a sail, a sail re-echoed from every part of the settlement.

A ship had been contracted for, with Mr. Bampton, from India about a year ago, the return of which was hourly expected; we had also hopes of the Daedalus, from the North West Court of America--She had left England with a cargo of provisions, and articles of traffic, and joined Captain Vancoover at Nootka Sound.--After having delivered what articles the Discovery and Chatham could at that time take on board; she was dispatched to this port, with that part of her cargo which was destined for us; and such stock as she might be able to procure from the islands she might touch at in her passage; Captain Vancoover requiring that she should join him again. On their passage out, the agent of Transports, Mr. Hergist, was unfortunately killed, with Mr. Gootch, an astronomer, who was going to join Captain Vancoover, at Whahoo, one of the Sandwich islands.

These people are described by Mr. Mears, in his Voyages, as a very--quiet inoffensive people, which description begat a confidence in them, so that they went on shore unarmed; the savages no sooner had them in their possession than they fell upon them, and most inhumanly murdered them. An armed party was sent from the ship but too late; for the two gentlemen were already massacred, and the horrid cannibals were preparing to broil and eat them; however, they drove them into the woods, and gathering the mangled limbs together, buried them on the beach.

A boat with an officer was sent down the harbour, and returned in the evening with the information that a ship under English colours had stood a considerable way into the bay, but being headed by a violent squall, she split her foretop sail, and was compelled again to put to sea. It was certain that the ship must be a stranger; for had any person on board had any knowledge of the harbour, they might with great safety have run her into Spring Cove; the sea running very high the officer could not board her without the most imminent danger.

As it grew dark the gale encreased, and morning was anxiously expected, but it produced us nothing but disappointment and uncertainty; we saw no more of her on that day, but the wind veering about to the great joy of every individual in the settlement, she hove in sight again no Monday the 10th. about three o'Clock in the afternoon, and at six she came safely to an anchor; as did the Arthur, a small brig from Bengal.

This ship proved to be the William, from Cork, with a cargo of beef and pork, but not an ounce of flour; though to make amends, she brought several pair of millstones, and a machine for dressing flour & c. which to us was a valuable acquisition and the very day after they were landed, Wilkinson's new mill was set to work; at first it went rather heavily, but in a few days, with the labour of nine men, ground a bushel of wheat in less than twenty minutes; previous to this there was no mill in the colony; the military as well as the convicts were obliged to make the best shift they could to render it into flour.

The brig had on board a small quantity of beef and pork, some sugar, rum, and coarse calicos--To our great surprise she brought no news of Mr. Bampton; nor had there been an account of his arrival at any of the ports in India. When he sailed from this place he expressed his determination of attempting a passage between this country and new Guinea. The navigation through this passage is mentioned as the most dangerous ever performed by any navigator; it had been passed by captain Blygh, and he was twenty days running thro' the passage. One day coming to an anchor to avoid danger, the Providence broke two of her anchors; and at last brought up near the shore, when eight canoes daringly attacked her, and killed and wounded several of her people--some of these canoes were seventy feet long, and contained six and twenty persons. To the disappointment which the colony sustained from the failure of the contracts already mentioned, for cattle and provisions; these accounts alarmed every one for Mr. Bampton's safety, and they feared that his ship had been wrecked on some of those shoals with which the streights abound, and that his officers and people had fallen a sacrifice to the natives.

In consequence of these fortunate arrivals, full allowance of salt meat was issued; and as soon as the cargoes were landed, the former deficiencies of allowance were made up to every individual. On the 17th. the last of the wheat was served, a proper quantity being reserved for seed, and on the next serving day, ten pounds of Indian corn were substituted for the allowance of wheat; although it was not yet ripe, and quite unfit to grind; the issuing it in this state was a matter of necessity. Had the settlers returned the wheat which they had received from government to sow their grounds last season, no such necessity would have existed; and it was certainly their duty to have stepped forward at this moment to assist the colony; but though they all knew the anxiety that prevailed to preserve the seed wheat, yet when applied to, they all pleaded that they had not sufficient to sow their grounds for the present season--This plea was well known to be without the least shadow of truth; In consequence, the governor ordered all those whose time of being victualled had expired, to be struck off the list, and left to provide for themselves, a punishment which they richly deserved--some of them had been permitted to receive their rations for more than a year after their EIGHTEEN MONTHS had expired--the term specified by government.

The distresses of the colony did not seem to make any amendment in the morals of the convicts. Gambling still prevailed among them to its fullest extent. One of the overseers, very much addicted to this ruinous passion, had given great offence to some of the prisoners, whereupon they formed a plan to rob him the first time he was observed to be favoured by fortune. He was accordingly surrounded one evening when at play, and having won a hazard of twenty five dollars, they rushed upon him as he was gathering up the stake, and secured the whole. He was fortunate enough to seize one of them with ten of the dollars in his hand, but lost the remainder. The offender was one who some time since had been reprieved at the foot of the gallows; he instantly received a severe corporal punishment, and the overseer, Mc. Koy, a sharp reprimand; in extenuation, he confessed that gaming had been his profession for many years, and that had it not been for this vice he should never have visited this country in the degrading situation of a convict.

In the month of April the Daedalus returned from Nootka, by her we learnt that Captain Vancoover had been to Whahoo, and that three of the natives had been delivered to him by the chief of the island, for the purpose of being sacrificed to the manes of Mr. Gootch and Lieutenant Hergist. The poor devils, asert remaining some time on board the Discovery, were taken one by one into a canoe, and put to death along--side the ship, by one of the chiefs, with a pistol; the effects of which equally astonished the executioner and the spectators.

One of the natives of Port Jackson, who had taken the name of Collins, had conceived a friendship for Lieut. Hanson, and had made the voyage with him. On his return to Sydney he found his wife in the possession of another, a very fine young fellow, called by us Wyatt, `The news of Collins' return and his being cloathed like us, drew many of his countrymen about him, and his rival among the rest; they surveyed each other with contemptuous sullenness, while the poor wife appeared greatly terrified; undetermined which to claim as her protector, suspecting that she should be the sufferer whether she was to belong to her former or her present husband. The point was soon determined--

they shivered a spear together, and Wyatt, who was wounded in the contest, was obliged to yield up the lady to her former lord, who, after having asserted his right by the force of arms, appeared indifferent about the reward, and was seen soon after traversing the country in quest of another wife.

Some of the natives perceiving that we were desirous of other fresh water rivers besides the Hawksbury, assured us that at a small distance from Botany Bay there was a large river which ran into the sea. Accordingly two of the soldiers who could be depended on, were sent from the South shore of Botany Bay, well armed; with provisions for a week.--A young man, a native, went with them as a guide; he professed a thorough knowledge of the country, and named the place where the fresh water was to be found; however, after a ramble of six days they returned it appeared that he had soon walked beyond his knowledge, and trusted to the soldiers to bring him back. Having penetrated about twenty miles to the Southward of Botany Bay they came to a pretty deep bay, which they went round; but discovered no traces of fresh water. The native evinced no disappointment, but returned as cheerfully and as well pleased as if he had led them to the banks of the finest river in the world. An Irish attorney, a convict, about this time planned an excursion of a different nature; which was to seize one of the long boats, and in her endeavour to find his way to Batavia. There were about a dozen concerned, and they had procured a quantity of provisions; casks, sails, and many other necessary articles were provided, and when the discovery was made were found in the the house of the principal. As there were no seamen among them, it was very lucky that they were prevented from putting to sea; as during the night they were to sail, it blew a violent gale of wind, and they must all have inevitably gone to the bottom. All that government had to regret in these desertions was the loss of the boats; for the colony would not sustain any injury from the evasion of a few malcontents, who were too idle to labour, and constantly promulgating their own seditious opinions among the other convicts.

Wilkinson the mill-wright was drowned in a pond which he ventured into after a duck he had shot, and getting entangled among the weeds, disappeared, though he was an expert swimmer, and there were several settlers by, who had been with him on the party, but could give him no assistance.

This unfortunate man was brought out in the Neptune as a convict, and had worked undistinguished among his fellow prisoners near three years, before it was discovered that he possessed any mechanical talents; nor very probably would they ever have been known, had they not been called forth by a desire of rivalling a mill-wright, of the name of Thorpe, who had been sent out by government.

He accordingly, having gained permission, set about a mill, the principal wheel of which was fifteen feet in diameter, and was worked by two men. This attempt being in direct opposition to the government mill--wright, consequently he could derive no assistance from his knowledge and abilities; and he had not only to contend with his opinions but of all those whom he could prejudice against him. The most laborious work, of cutting and preparing the timber, was performed by his fellow prisoners, who voluntarily gave him their labour. It took him upwards of three months before it was offered for trial, when it proved defective, owing to the timber not being properly seasoned; however the projector was found to possess great merit, and had the whole been conctructed on a larger scale it would no doubt have answered his most sanguine expectations. Perceiving what were the defects of his first essay, he undertook to make one on an improved plan, which he was prevented from completing by his untimely death.

Some daring villains, returning evil for good, broke into the house of the Reverend Mr. Johnston, and robbed him of various articles to a very considerable amount: his servants were suspected (and no doubt justly) of being accessary, as the part they entered was the store room, and only known to those about the house. Several people were taken up, and some of the articles found in the woods, but those who committed the robbery had the address to elude a discovery. Another daring burglary was committed in a house occupied by Mr. Kent, agent for the convicts, he had secured the door with a strong padlock, and after sun-set had gone out to spend the evening. About nine o'clock word was brought him that his house had been broken open; on going home he found that the staple had been wrenched off, and a large chest, a load for four men, had been carried away. It contained a large quantity of wearing apparel; money, bills, letters, & c. and although the robbery could not have been perpetrated more than an hour or two, no traces of it could be found, although a great number of people spent the greater part of the night in searching after them; the chest and a very small part of its contents was found the next morning. A highway robbery was also committed about the same time on the person of an American Supercargo. He was attacked in the dusk of the evening by two men, close by the barracks; as they struck him they seized hold of his watch, and with a violent jerk tore away the seals; the watch falling on the ground, and the place being too public for them to stay to look for it, they decamped with the seals only.

Notwithstanding every precaution, the horrid vice of gaming (the parent of these enormities) still prevailed, from the address and management with which it was carried on.--The persons of the peace--officers were known to them, and that they might not be detected in the fact, one of the party, each in their turn, was stationed to look out, and give the alarm.

In the second year of the settlement, it was reported that a man was found murdered in one of the coves, a short distance from the settlement; a general muster of the convicts thereupon took place, but no person was absent except Caesar, a black fellow, who had absconded a few days before, from the service of one of the officers, and taken to the woods with some provisions, an iron pot and a musket. Robberies being very frequent after Caesar's flight, parties were sent after him who at length with some difficulty brought him in. He was reputed the hardest working man in the country; his body was muscular, and well calculated for hard labour; but in his intellects he was not far removed from the brute creation; his appetite was so ravenous that he could devour the full ration of three days in one; to pamper this appetite he was compelled to steal from others;--and this he did at every opportunity, without even caring for the consequences; indeed he was so indifferent about being punished with death, that he used to declare if they should scrag him he would quiz them all, and show them some gig at the nubbing-cheat, before he was turned off. The governor did not think him a proper object to make an example of, therefore ordered that he should be kept at work in fetters; however, he contrived to free himself from them, and several times got off to the woods, but was generally soon taken, and a severe flogging was always the result; and which he always treated with the utmost contempt. In one of his excursions, he quarrelled with and killed one of the natives called Pemulwy, who had some time before wounded Collins, a great favourite with the colonists; he requested his friends to take him to the hospital, and when he was brought thither, it was found that a barbed spear had been driven into his loins, close to the vertebrae of the back, and was so firmly fixed that all the efforts of the Surgeons to remove it with their instruments were in-effectual. Finding that he could not be relieved by art, he determined to trust to their general Physician and Surgeon, Nature, and he did not trust in vain; for some weeks he was seen walking about with the spear unmoved, even after the wound had suppurated, but at last after many fruitless efforts, his wife Warreweer, succeeded, and drew it out with her teeth, after which he quickly recovered.

The many robberies that were nightly committed, rendered it expedient to put a stop to an evil so destructive of the happiness and comfort of the industrious inhabitants, Caesar was still in the woods, with several other vagabonds, all of whom were armed, and as the savage had declared that he would never suffer himself to be taken alive, it became absolutely necessary to secure such a desperado, at all events. A proclamation was accordingly issued, promising to whomsoever should bring him in, with his arms, a reward of five gallons of spirits; and those who were indulged with ammunition by the officers, were informed that if they should be discovered in supplying the plunderers and run aways with any part of it, they would be deemed accomplices in the robberies, and punished accordingly.

This proclamation had not the desired effect, Black Caesar continued to elude all his pursuers; and scarcely a day past but complaints of robberies were preferred against him. In short every theft that was committed was ascribed to him; a cask of pork was stolen from the mill-house, the upper part of which was accessible; the centinels who had charge of the building were tried and acquitted, and the theft was laid upon Caesar, or some of the vagabonds in the woods, the number of whom at this time amounted to near a dozen.

This ruffian continued his lawless and predatory reign till the 15th. of February 1796, when he was shot by one Wimbow. This man and another, allured by the reward, had been some time in search of him; having found his haunt, a cavern, the mouth of which was covered with short thick brush wood, which rendered it almost imperceptible; they dogged him, and saw him enter it in the dusk of the evening; they hid themselves near it all night. In the morning, when he turned out of his den, he looked round, and seeing his danger, presented his piece; ere he could pull the trigger, Wimbow fired and shot him--he was taken to the house of Rose, the settler, at Liberty Plains, where he died in a few hours--Thus was the colony at length rescued from the depredations of a ruffian, whom no indulgence could reclaim, nor severity intimidate.

Chapter IX.

About the middle of July 1794 arrived the Fancy, Snow, from Bombay, with a part of the provisions contracted for with Captain Bampton, who had arrived at Bombay after a tedious voyage of near seven months. Mr. Thomas Dell, formerly chief mate of the Shah Hormuzear, commanded this vessel; from him we were informed of the following particulars of that disastrous voyage. The Shah Hormuzear, in company with the Chesterfield, sailed from Norfolk Island on the 27th. of May 1793--On the First of July they fell in with an island which they called Tate's Island.--Captain Hill, of the New South Wales Corps, with Mr. Carter, had taken their passage to Europe in this ship--Mr. Shaw, chief mate of the Chesterfield, with a boat's crew went on shore for fresh provisions; they purposed staying all night on the Island to barter for emu feathers. They had scarce landed when it came on to blow, and the ship was driven considerably to leeward of the bay.

The natives received the gentlemen very kindly, and appeared highly gratified with the presents which they severally made them. It was now proposed that Mr. Carter, Mr. Shaw and Ascott--the convict whose activity preserved the Sirius from being destroyed by Fire, the night she went on shore at Norfolk Island--should proceed to the top of a high point of land which was at some distance; and that Captain Hill should stay by the boat, with her crew; four seamen belonging to the Chesterfield.

The party proceeding in-land had taken the precaution of arming themselves. Nothing particular occurred during their walk, though some trifling circumstances induced Ascott to suspect that the Natives meditated some mischievous design against them; this idea he imparted to his companions, who scouted his apprehensions. On their return from the hill, their designs became more apparent, and the savages seemed only deterred from committing violence on them by the activity of Ascott, who frequently presented his musket at them to keep them off, but notwithstanding his activity and vigilance they at length made their attack. They first attempted to make themselves master of Ascott's gun, finding him the most likely to annoy them; directly after which Mr. Carter, who was the foremost of the party, suddenly exclaimed "My God, My God! they have murdered me." Ascott, who still retained his gun, instantly fired, on which the Natives left them and fled into the bushes. Ascott now came to the spot where he saw a most dreadful spectacle; Mr. Carter lying bleeding on the ground, and Mr. Shaw with a large wound on his throat under the left jaw. They were however able to rise and proceed down to the boat. On their arrival at the beach they called out to their companions to fire; but to their extreme horror they perceived Captain Hill and one of the seamen lying dead on the sand, cut and mangled in the most barbarous manner. Two others of the seamen they saw floating on the water, with their throats cut from ear to ear,--the fourth sailor they found dead in the boat, mangled in the same shocking manner. With much difficulty these unhappy people got into their boat, and, cutting her grapnel, pulled off from this treacherous Island. While they were getting out of the bay, they perceived the natives dragging the bodies of Captain Hill and the seamen from the beach towards some large fires, which they supposed were prepared for the occasion; yelling and howling at the same time dismally.

These wretched survivors of their companions, having seen from the top of the hill, whither their ill fated curiosity had led them, a large sand bank, not far from the island, determined to run under the lee of it, as they very reasonably expected that boats would be sent from the ship in search of them. They experienced very little ease or rest that night, and when day light appeared found that they had drifted nearly out of sight of the island, and to leeward of the sand bank.

Finding it was impossible to reach the bank, they determined by the advice of Shaw, the only seaman among them, to run direct for Timor, the wind being very luckily fair for that settlement. On examining what was left in the boat, they found a few of the trifles which they had taken to barter with the natives, and Ascott's great-coat, but neither compass, provisions, nor water. They however pushed on to the westward, trusting to that providence for their relief, which had delivered them from the treacherous cannibals at Tate's Island.

In this forlorn and destitute condition, weakened by the loss of blood, with scarce strength to manage the boat; their sufferings became almost too much for human nature to sustain before they reached a place of safety.

They left the island on the third of July; on the seventh two small birds dropped into the boat which they instantly devoured, and were considerably revived by this providential relief; on the next day they had the land on both sides of them, they passed through these streights, and continued their course to the westward. All that could be done with their wounds was to open them from time to time and cleanse them with salt water; on the eleventh they saw land a head of them, and in the afternoon pushed their boat into a small bay. Here they found the natives apparently very hospitable, giving them roasted Yams and fresh water, they also gave them to understand that Timor was still to the southward of them. Not considering themselves in perfect safety they again embarked; they had not gone far from the land when they perceived that they were chaced by a large Proa, which they escaped by standing over a reef which the Indians did not chuse to encounter. At day break on the 13th. they saw a point of land, but not being able to weather it, they ran into a small bay, where the natives received them, crying out "Bligh, Bligh." Here they landed, were hospitably entertained, and freed from the horror of perishing by famine.

This place was called by the natives Sarrett, and was distinct from Timor land, which was the first they refreshed at. They found also that there was another small island to the Northward, called by them Fardatte, but which is commonly called in charts, Tanabor, where a Proa comes yearly from Banda to trade, and which they expected in about seven or right months.

On the twenty-fifth of June Mr. Carter's wound was entirely healed, after having had thirteen pieces of the fractured skull taken out: but he did not long survive his cure,--he caught a fever on the seventeenth of November, and died on the tenth of December, much regretted by his two fellow sufferers. Mr. Shaw and Ascot waited, in anxious expectation, the arrival of the trading Proa from Banda, which, to their great joy, entered the harbour on the twelfth of March.

For Banda they sailed on the tenth of April, and arrived there on the first of May, where they were received with the greatest hospitality by the governor, who supplied them with every necessary that they wanted, and provided them with a passage on board an Indiaman bound to Batavia, where they landed on the tenth of October.

To return to the Ships; the boats had but scarcely landed, when it came on to blow, and increased to a gale, so that the ships were driven several leagues to leeward of the bay in which they landed; and it was three days before they could send any boats in search of them--Mr. Dell, and a party well armed, search'd in vain for them; and burned several huts of the natives--At a place where there had been a fire they had incontestible proofs that their friends had fallen sacrifices to the inhuman cruelty of the natives--three human hands, their great coats with the buttons cut off; a tinder-box, a lanthorn, a tomahawk, and other articles from the boat were also found. They rowed entirely round the island, searching in vain for their boat; they endeavoured to make some of the natives prisoners but without effect; they, however, made them understand by signs that they had murdered all who were in the boat, except two, who got away with her--he was therefore obliged to return on board with the meancholy account.

The island is described as abounding with sweet potatoes, bananas, plantains, bamboo, cocoa trees, and mangroves; the natives stout, and from five feet eight inches to six feet two in height; their colour dark, and their language harsh and disagreeable. Their weapons are spears, lances of hard black wood, and clubs about four feet in length. They live in huts, resembling a haycock, with a pole driven through the middle, formed of long grass and the leaves of the cocoa tree; and many contain six or eight persons each: they are enclosed with a strong piece of bamboo. In a corner of some of the huts were perceived a wooden image, intended to represent a man; in others the figure of a bird, very rudely carved, daubed with red ochre, and curiously decorated with the feathers of the emu. Over these images were suspended, from the roof, several strings of human hands, each string having five or six hands on it. In some they found small piles of human skulls; and in one, in which there was a larger pile than in any other that they had visited; they observed some gum burning before a wooden image. The island was supposed to be about fifteen miles in circumference, in Longitude one hundred and forty two degrees fifty nine minutes East of Greenwich.--The Shah Hormuzear did not arrive at Timor until the eleventh of September, having been detained in the straits by a most difficult and dangerous navigation.

Chapter X.

The rogues who had broken into Mr. Kent's house had the audacity to send him a letter in miserable verse, containing some accusations against Bevan, who was at present in confinement for a felony, and a woman who they supposed had given information of the people that broke into the clergyman's store-room, of which they acknowledged themselves to have been the perpetrators; the letter was accompanied with a pocket book belonging to Mr. Kent with some memorandums, but not, one of the bills that were in it were ever recovered.

This daring proceeding, and the frequency of their nightly depredations obliged every person to be on their guard and to keep a strict look-out, 'till at length three convicts were apprehended on suspicion of house--breaking, and were accordingly brought to trial--John Bevan, was acquitted for want of evidence, the other two John Fleming, and Archibald Macdonald were capitally convicted; they had broken into a soldier's hut, and were said to have been concerned in robbing Mr. Johnstone. They were executed on the third day after the trial.

In the month of August 1794, a party of half a dozen of us set out in search of stragglers, of which there were a great number in the woods, and took provisions for a week's excursion, after proceeding a few miles inland we came to a ridge of mountains, very difficult of ascent, and when at the top our prospect was bounded by another ridge with an intermediate valley of about a mile across; in this valley we took up our first nights lodging in a sort of hut which had been the occasional shelter of some of the hunters tribe; we kindled a fire and kept watch by turns till day-break, when we proceeded on our journey, and were not a little surprised when we had ascended the second ridge, to find another still before us at about the same distance, in short we passed seventeen or eighteen of these ridges in the same manner; at last we despaired of penetrating beyond the mountains and determined on returning, having been according to computation sixty miles from the settlement, and twenty miles farther in the country than any person had yet ventured.

The summit of these rocks are iron stone, large fragments of which lay scattered in the valleys, in which were ponds of water with a reddish tinge,--the soil on the ascent was tolerably good and afforded shelter for large herds of the red Kangaroo.--The valleys bore visible signs of being frequently visited by high winds or hurricanes, and were strewed by trunks of trees: we saw but few of the natives who fled at our approach, and seemed to prefer the enjoyment of rocks and woods to any intercourse with us: we returned to Paramatta after a most toilsome journey of nine days, and without obtaining the least satisfaction in our researches.

The Irish prisoners were now again become very troublesome; and several of them missing muster, it was instantly rumoured that they had formed a plan to seize the Cumberland, a large decked-boat, which had lately sailed with provisions for the settlers at the Hawksbury river. Some went so far as to say that she was already taken just without the point of the harbour. Notice was immediately dispatched over land, to the settlement on the river to put the people in the boat on their guard against a surprize; and for them to return to Port Jackson the instant that her cargo was delivered. An armed long boat was also sent to protect her in her passage back.

A few days relieved us from suspence with regard to the Cumberland, as all the reports were without any foundation; and were most probably fabricated to conceal a different scheme which, while every one's attention was taken up with the fate of the Cumberland, they actually put in execution.

Some of these Hibernian gentry stole a six oared boat, belonging to Lieutenant Mc Arthur, with which they got clear of the harbour undiscovered; but some days after she was found at Botany Bay.--The people threatned resistance, but soon took to the woods, leaving the boat with all the things they had prepared for their voyage. They soon appeared, at the farms about Sydney, for plunder, but one of them being fired at and wounded, the rest thought it would be most prudent to surrender themselves which they accordingly did. They confessed that they never meant to return, but wanted to go to Broken bay, which they thought they had reached when they arrived at Botany Bay, being entirely ignorant of its situation or whether it lay to the northward, or the southward. The wounded man died the next day in the hospital, and his companions after a severe flogging, were sent to their respective gangs to labour with an Iron on each of their legs.

About this time a public granary at Paramatta was burnt down, but whether owing to incendiaries, or accident was never known, the loss was very considerable, near three thousand bushels of wheat, and a quantity of stock belonging to individuals also perished in the flames.

The natives about the Hawksbury now began to quarrel with the settlers, and took every opportunity of pil-fearing from them; becoming more bold from not meeting with a check, half a dozen of them stole unawares upon one of the settlers, wounded him and his servant and got them in their power before they could procure any assistance. The servant was so severely hurt with spears and clubs that his life was endangered,--encouraged by this first essay, they a few days after in a stronger party attacked the huts while the settlers were in their grounds at work and was carrying off all their cloaths, provisions, and whatever they could lay their hands on, the alarm being given, the sufferers collected what arms they could, and attacked the murderers in a body, and killed seven or eight of them on the spot.

It was generally supposed that the settlers had drawn these evils upon themselves by their own misconduct: there was not a doubt but that many natives had been wantonly fired upon; and whenever they could get any of their children into their possession would detain them, notwithstanding the earnest entreaties of their parents to return them.

In the autumn of 1794 warrants of emancipation passed the great seal of the settlement, in behalf of Robert Sidaway, who received an unconditional pardon, in consideration of his diligence, good conduct, and strict integrity in his employment for several years, as the public baker of the settlement; and William Leach, who was permitted to quit the country, provided he did not return to England till the term of his transportation was expired. Eight were permitted to list in the New South Wales Corps, and James Harris, James Ruffler, and Richard Partridge, who were all transported for life, received a pardon, or (according to their own term) were made free on the ground, which enabled them to become settlers, as were also William Joyce, Benjamin Carver, and William Waring.

Two female natives, the sisters of Banalang and his fellow traveller, having applied to the Lieutenant Governor to defend them from the insults and cruelties they frequently experienced from their countrymen in the absence of their protectors; were sent on board the Daedalus to be taken to Norfolk Island, where they would spend their time in peace and retirement, under the protection of Captain King, till the return of their brothers.

John Bevan, who has been several times made mention of, was tried on the first of October, for breaking open the house of William Fielder, a settler at Sydney, and being caught in the fact, was fully convicted, and received sentence of death; and at nine in the morning of the sixth he was executed. The night previous to this execution, a murder was committed at Parramatta by one Hill, a convict, on the body of Simon Burns a free settler. It appeared on the trial, which lasted five hours that Hill, a butcher by trade, had lived in a state of continued animosity with the deceased, taking every opportunity of abusing and quarrelling with him,--they had been out drinking in company all Sunday;--a woman who lived with Hill coming in, words arose between them, and Hill rising to strike her, she ran out of the house to avoid a beating;--the deceased interfering was stabbed by Hill to the heart; he lived a very few minutes, and had but just strength to declare in the presence of several witnesses, that the butcher had killed him. The prisoner attempted to establish an alibi, but the fact was clearly proved against him, and he was sentenced to die, and his body to be dissected, which was accordingly performed on the 16th.

A very serious complaint was made by the natives (through the medium of some who lived at Sydney, and could speak English tolerably) against the Settlers at the Hawkesbury, which corroborated the opinion before stated. It was now asserted, that some of them had seized a native boy, and, tying him hand and foot, had dragged him several times over a fire, till his back was dreadfully burnt; after which they threw him into the river, where they shot at, and killed him. A strict investigation of this complaint immediately took place, when it came out, that a boy had been actually shot by them when he was in the water, but that they had considered him as a spy, detached from a large body of the natives, who had assembled with an intention of falling on them; and that he was returning to them with an account of their weakness, there being only one musket among several farms. These assertions being uncontradicted, they were admitted as truths; but it was conjectured by many only to be a fabrication, invented to cover the true circumstance,--that a boy had been cruelly and wantonly murdered by them.

An action at civil law was brought by Joyce, the convict who had lately received his freedom, against Thomas Davenny, a superintendant of convicts at Toongabbe, when the defendant availed himself of a misnomer; the plea being admitted, the plaintiff was nonsuited, and before the next court assembled, the parties compromised the business.

Chapter XI.

On the 25th of October, Messrs Muir; Palmer, Skirving, and Margorott, four gentlemen, arrived in the Surprise transport. They had been tried in Scotland for sedition, were convicted, and transported to this country. They were each allowed a small neat house and garden, with servants to wait on them.

Mr. Muir was tried before the High Court of Justiciary in Edinburgh, on the 20th of August, 1793. He was accused of exciting, at different meetings, denominated Societies of Reform, by means of seditious speeches and harangues, a spirit of disaffection against the King and Government--of producing and reading aloud "An Address from the United Irishmen in Dublin, to the Delegates for promoting a Reform in Scotland;" and of circulating and distributing such seditious writings. To these charges Mr. Muir pleaded Not Guilty. He said, he had nothing to observe on the relevancy; he would trust himself to the Jury. He had given in a written defence, in which he declared the libel to be false, and that he would prove that he had all along supported the constitution. Being asked if he had any other defence; he said, he rested upon his own written defence. He had uniformly advised the people to pursue legal and constitutional measures, as well as to read all works written upon the great national question of reform. The Jury being named, Mr. Muir objected to every one of them; he said, that as the gentlemen were all subscribers of the Goldsmiths' Hall Association, and had offered a reward for discovering those who circulated what they were pleased to term seditious publications, they had already prejudged him, and were therefore improper persons to pass upon his assize. The Solicitor--General, in reply, said, their Lordships were equally precluded, as both they, and every friend to the constitution, had condemned the writings of Paine.--After examining the witnesses in behalf of the prosecution, and the prisoner, the Lord Justice Clerk summed up the evidence, and after commenting in very strong language on the different parts of it, left the Jury to draw their own conclusions; who bringing in their verdict guilty, the Court sentenced him to be transported beyond the seas, to such place as his Majesty, with the advice of his Privy Council, should judge proper, for the space of fourteen years.--Mr. Muir observed, that though some in the Court might think the sentence too lenient, and others too severe, yet had he been taken from the bar to the scaffold, he would have met his fate with equal coolness, so convinced was he of the justice of his cause.--Mr. Palmer, who was a Clergyman, was tried at Perth, found guilty of writing a seditious hand-bill, and his sentence was seven years transportation. Messrs. Margarot and Skirving were tried for the same practices, and were sentenced to fourteen years each.

By this ship we heard that his Excellency was on his passage, and might be very soon expected. As soon as the store ships were cleared, a general distribution of slops took place among the convicts; to the men, a jacket, waistcoat; shirt, hat, and a pair of breeches; and to the women, one petticoat, one shift, one pair of stockings, one cap, one neck kerchief, one hat, and one jacket, made of raven duck. A distinction was made with respect to the overseers and watchmen, who received a coat instead of a jacket, duck trowsers instead of breeches, and one pair of shoes.

Several seamen belonging to a ship bound to the North-west coast of America, preferring the pleasures which they met with on shore in the society of the women, and the free circulation of grog, to proceeding on their voyage, left their ship some days previous to her sailing. Application being made the Lieutenant-Governor, orders were issued out to apprehend them; they were also given to understand, that if they remained behind they would be severely punished, and kept to hard labour; but the settlements now had become so extensive, that runaways and vagrants never failed of finding employment in the remote parts, more particularly at the river.

Towards the close of the year, a farm of five and twenty acres of ground was sold by public auction for thirteen pounds; four acres were planted with Indian corn, and half an acre with potatoes; there was besides a tolerable hut on the premises. This farm was the property of Samuel Crane, a soldier, who received his death by a tree falling on him, which he was felling.

Lieutenant-Governor Grose embarked for England in the Daedalus, on the 15th of December, with several gentlemen of the colony, and some convicts, whose terms had expired. The command now was vested in Captain William Paterson, senior officer in the colony, and he took the prescribed oaths accordingly.

Many of the convicts' terms were now expired; numbers also, by their good conduct, had obtained their emancipation, and were at liberty to work for themselves: the officers and settlers had also a considerable number in their employ, so that the public agriculture was nearly at a stand. Captain Paterson, therefore, caused a general muster to take place, and upwards of fifty people were found without any employment, whose labour still belonged to the public; most of these were laid hold of, and sent to Parramatta and Toongabbe, with a large gang of labourers, to prepare the public grounds for wheat for the ensuing season. They began their work on the 2nd, of January, New Year's Day being always kept as a holiday.

It was now determined to station some military force at the Hawkesbury settlement, as well to preserve good order and regulation among the settlers, as to defend them against the natives; accordingly a schooner was dispatched with an officer and a guard; they had also a mill, and provisions for the settlers.

A convict, on entering his hut, was bit on the foot by a black snake; an immediate swelling took place up to his hip, and a large tumour in the groin. Mr. Thompson, the surgeon, reduced all the swellings, by frequently bathing the parts with oil, and fortunately saved both the man's life and the limb also. Before the settlement was cleared from the wood, snakes and other reptiles were by no means so frequently seen as since; by clearing and opening the woods they were not destroyed by fire, but now they were often seen basking in the foot-paths at mid-day, particularly after a shower of rain.

The principal labour performed in January was preparing the ground for wheat. The Indian corn looked remarkably well; it was now ripening, and the Hawkesbury settlers supposed that they should have between thirty and forty thousand bushels of that grain raised among themselves. Allured by the civil treatment they experienced, several native boys had taken up their quarters among the settlers in the several districts, and became extremely useful; thay laboured cheerfully in the fields, and performed more of that kind of labour in a few hours, than a convict would in a whole day.

The store-house on the Hawkesbury being finished, the stores from the schooner were landed, and put under the care of Baker, the settler; several of the officers had come round with the schooner, with a view of selecting eligible spots for farms; on their return, they spoke in very high terms of the crops of corn which they saw growing there--the generality of the farms that had been in wheat, producing from thirty-six to forty bushels an acre; that a bushel was sufficient to sow an acre; and that, if sown as early as April, the ground would produce a second harvest. Their gardens are abundantly stocked with vegetable.

A wild young fellow, named Wilson, whose term of servitude had expired, preferred the mode of living among the natives, to earning his livelihood by the sweat of his brow. This person acquainted the settlers that the natives had threatened to put some of them to death: which caution made them vigilant and on their guard However, they attacked and wounded two of them.

The tribe with which Wilson associated had given him the name of Bunboe; as he was of a thoughtless, dissipated disposition, and his sole view of herding with them was merely to prevent his being obliged to work for his living, no good consequence was supposed could accrue from his conduct; and it was not improbable: but that, at some future period, he might assist them in their deprecations on the settlers.

The Deputy Surveyor-General, Mr. Grimes, having received orders to take the schooner, as soon as she had delivered her cargo, to Port Stephens; for the purpose of taking a regular survey of that harbour; this Wilson, or Bunboe, being a useful fellow on such occasions, having a slight smattering of the native tongue, was prevailed on to go with him. On their arrival at Port Stephens they found two fresh-water branches; they did not run far up the river, but terminated in a swamp not far from the beach. Mr. Grimes describes the land on each side to be low and sandy, and found nothing which could render a second visit necessary. The natives were far from being friendly; they appeared rather a taller and stouter race than those about this settlement, and their language entirely different. Their canoes and huts were considerably larger than those we had seen here, but their weapons were the same. They were welcomed on shore with a dance, joined hand in hand round a tree, probably to express their unanimity; but one of them making signs for Mr. Grimes to follow him into the wood, which he had no sooner entered than he poised a spear, and was on the point of throwing it, when Wilson, who had watched his motions, levelled a double barrelled gun at him, and fired; he instantly dropped, and it was thought he was wounded, but he presently jumped up and prepared a second time to throw the spear, when Wilson gave him the fire he had in reserve, which took effect, and he was seen to rise no more. Mr. Grimes now made the best of his way to the boat, which he reached without further molestation.

The 17th of March St. Patrick found many votaries in the settlement, and the late arrivals from the Cape had made brandy very plentiful;--the libations to the Saint were proportionably liberal; so that riot and debauchery, for the space of four and twenty hours, were the order of the day.

A few days after the feast of St. Patrick, having some business at Sydney, and passing the brick fields, I saw, at the lower end of the second field, one of the native women in close conference with a young man; an amorous scene ensued, which was soon interrupted by the appearance of a third person, who proved to be the lord and master of the lady, who lay panting in the embraces of another. She instantly took to flight, and escaped for the time, but the lover was not so fortunate, for the enraged husband, being much more powerful than his antagonist, literally beat him to death, before we could arrive at the spot to his rescue. The friends of the deceased called Goruey to an account for the murder, and the affair being conducted with more regard to punctilio than justice, he came off with a slight wound in his thigh.

Amongst various other burglaries, the house of Mr. Muir was broken into, and nearly all that gentleman's property stolen; some articles were laid in his way the next day, but he remained a very considerable loser by the visit. The private stock yards were frequently attacked, but a pretty sharp look out being generally kept, they seldom met with much success in those attempts. One fellow played off a trick that he thought would go down with the hungry; he stole a very fine greyhound, and, instead of keeping him to hunt, killed him secretly, and sold the flesh to different people for kangaroo, at nine-pence per pound, but being detected, he received a most exemplary punishment,--a just reward for his villainy.

A criminal court having been assembled on the 20th of May, Mary Pawson was tried for the crime of arson. On the trial it appeared that the prisoner bore a most implacable hatred to the wife of the owner of the house that was burnt, but there was no evidence that directly led to convict her of having set the house on fire. She was accordingly acquitted; but the settlers adjoining their farm, disliking such a character in their neighbourhood, obliged the husband, who was an honest man, and had nothing against him but his wife, to sell a very good farm, and go to a more remote and less advantageous situation. At the same time, James Barry, a notorious offender, was tried for attempting to break into a settler's house at the Ponds, with an intent to steal; the proof was too clear to admit of his escape. He was sentenced to receive a thousand lashes.

Bunboe, directly after his return from Port Stephens, went off to the natives at the river. Another vagabond like himself, Knight, thinking there must be much pleasure in the roving life which Wilson led, determined to go off with him; they had not been gone long when they both returned into the town, accompanied by some of their companions. On the following day it appeared that this visit was for the purpose of forcing a wife from among the women of this district, agreeably to the custom of the country. They accordingly selected two girls, the eldest not twelve years old, whom they seized, and, assisted by their friends, were hurrying off with them. The shrieks of the children soon brought assistance, who rescued them, and took their ravishers, who were severely punished; but though a strict guard was kept over them, they soon found means to elude their vigilance, and joined their former companions.

Chapter XII.

On the 20th of August, his Majesty's ship Providence, Captain Broughton, arrived from England, with the agreeable intelligence that they had left Governor Hunter, in the Reliance, at Rio Janeiro, and that he might be hourly expected. The Providence had missed this port, and was driven as far to the northward as Port Stephens, where, to the great surprise of Captain Broughton, he found four runaways from this settlement; they were so covered with filth, tanned by the sun, and dried by the smoke, that they were absolutely taken for natives. They were found to be Tarwood, Lee, Connoway, and Watson. These men,--with Joseph Sutton, since dead,--in the night of the 26th of September 1790, stole a small punt, with which they got down to Sydney; they there exchanged the punt for a boat, with a mast and sail, with which they got clear of the harbour. They had each taken provisions for a week, their clothes, bed and bedding, their iron pots, and several kitchen utensils. These desperate adventurers had been universally supposed to have been swallowed up by the ocean, or perished with hunger. They now told a melancholy tale of their sufferings in the boat, and for many days after their arrival, had crowds of both black and white people listening to the adventures which befel them in Port Stephens, Having been hospitably received by the savages, they fared as they did; but the change in their living soon disagreed with them, and they were all taken ill, and principally affected with swellings in the abdomen, but soon recovered, except Sutton, who fell a victim. They gave the natives a very high character for hospitality and kindness. Each of them had arms given to them, with very curious ceremonies; wives also were allotted them, and one or two had children. They were never required to interfere in their wars, and were supplied by the natives with fish, and other food, and really considered them as unfortunate strangers, who had a claim to their protection. They said that the natives appeared to worship them, telling them,--when they began to understand each other,--that they were undoubtedly the ancestors of some of them who had fallen in battle, and had returned from the sea to visit them again; and one of them firmly believed that his father was absolutely come back in the person of Lee, or Connoway, and took them to the spot where his body had been burnt. On being told that great numbers of people existed, far beyond their knowledge to conceive, they instantly pronounced them to be the spirits of their countrymen, which, after death, had migrated into other regions. It appeared, when Mr. Grimes was there, that they were at some distance inland; that they had heard of the schooner's being there, and were acquainted with the man who was shot by Wilson, who had afterwards recovered.

On the 7th of September, Governor Hunter arrived, but did not assume the exercise of his authority until the 11th, when his commission was publicly read by the Judge Advocate. His Excellency, in a very pertinent speech, declared the expectations he had from every one's conduct, touching with great delicacy on that of the gentlemen who had newly arrived from Scotland, and who were present; strongly urging the necessity of a general unanimity in support of his Majesty's Government. He was afterwards sworn in by the Judge Advocate, and a general act of oblivion extended throughout the settlement, whereby Raymond, who was under sentence of death, was pardoned, and several runaways returned to their labour.

The report of the general muster, made by order of Captain Paterson, being laid before the Governor, he thought proper to make some alterations in the assistance granted by Government to settlers, and others, holding allotments of land. To the officers, cultivating grounds, he continued the number they already had, viz. ten for agriculture, and three for domestic purposes. To the settlers he allowed five male convicts; to the superintendants, constables, and store-keepers, four; the marine settlers, two; to settlers who had been convicts, one; and to serjeants of the New South Wales corps, one.

On the 5th of November, the Sovereign store-ship arrived from England, in which was embarked Mr. Joseph Gerald, who was adjudged to fourteen years transportation, for being a member of a seditious club, or association called The British Convention, and for making addresses of a seditious tendency to the members of the said Convention. He arrived in a very weak and debilitated state of health. He languished about four months in the last stage of a consumption, and died on the 16th of March 1796. This gentleman was born in the West Indies, where he inherited considerable property. His first residence in England was under the roof of Doctor Parr, with whom he remained a number of years. When he returned to the West Indies he married a beautiful young lady, with a considerable fortune; by her he had two sons, with whom he went over to England to establish them at an academy, where they now are. Mrs. Gerald is still living in the West Indies. Three days after, he was followed by his companion, Mr. Skirving, who died of a dysentery. These gentlemen were much regretted by the whole colony; their political opinions never manifested themselves, and all their solicitude seemed to be to evince themselves the friends of human nature.

On the 7th of November a criminal court was held, when the following persons where tried:--Chinnery, a black, for robbing his master; Samuel Smith, and Abraham Whitehouse, for house-breaking: these were found guilty, and condemned to die. Two settlers and six convicts, for an assault, with intent to ravish Marianne Wilkinson, three of whom were found guilty, and sentenced as follows: The principal to receive one thousand lashes; the others eight hundred each. This was the second trial for this crime; but the witnesses prevaricated so much in the first instance, that the offenders, for that time, escaped punishment, which had encouraged several others to commit the same unmanly attacks, in numbers, on a single woman. To such a height was this infamous practice carried, that it obtained a cant name, and the poor unfortunate objects of this brutality,--many of whom, through shame, concealed the circumstance,--received a nickname, expressive of the injuries they received.

Several contests, which happened at this time among the natives, had brought many of the distant tribes down to Sydney, to be spectators; some of whom observing the cattle in the colony, said that they had seen many of the same kind in the woods. This intelligence getting to the Governor, he ordered a more particular enquiry to be made; and being satisfied as to the truth of the report, and their track being clearly ascertained, his Excellency determined to satisfy himself. He accordingly set off on the 27th of November with a strong party; having travelled three days in a S.S.W. direction from the settlement at Prospect Hill, he crossed Nepean river, and, to his great surprise and satisfaction, he fell in with a very fine herd of cattle, grazing in a rich luxuriant pasture. The day was too far advanced to make an accurate survey of them, so he halted for the night in a pleasant spot in the vicinity, expecting in the morning to be gratified with a sight of the whole herd. A doubt was started whether they were the progeny of those we had imported from the Cape, or whether they were not of a longer standing; his Excellency was therefore determined to satisfy their doubts, and accordingly directed some of the party to endeavour to kill one of the calves. This they were not able to effect; for, while lying in wait to let the herd pass, which now consisted of upwards of fourscore, they were furiously attacked by a young bull, which they were obliged to kill in their own defence, This, however, answered the purpose; for, as it was full grown, they had an opportunity of satisfying their doubts respecting their identity, as being the offspring of the cattle which were lost in June 1788. Being at this time near forty miles from any of the settlements, a very small quantity of the meat could be brought in; the remainder, to the great regret of the party, was left to be devoured by wild dogs, & c. The country where they were found grazing was remarkably pleasant; the group was richly covered with thick luxuriant grass; the trees were thinly scattered, and free from underwood: several large plots were embellished with ponds, covered with black swans and flocks of ducks, the margins of which were beautifully fringed with variegated shrubs, and the ground from these levels rose into hills of gradual and easy ascent.

How these cattle came hither was easily accounted for. The two bulls, and five cows, that strayed from the keeper in 1788, had travelled, without interruption, in a western direction, until they came to the banks of the river Nepean, where, finding the river fordable, they arrived in a country well watered, and plentifully supplied with rich pasture, from whence they had no inducement to remove; and where they remained unmolested, as none of the natives were found in their neighbourhood, and where they were likely to remain, undisturbed securely to propagate their species. The Governor, considering that it was of the greatest consequence to the colony that their numbers should not be diminished, and that, if permitted to continue thus in their wild state, they might hereafter, like the cattle on the Spanish main, not only prove sufficient for the consumption of the colony, but a source of commerce to the inhabitants; he was therefore determined, as much as in his power, to prevent any of them from being destroyed.

Bannalong, who returned with the Governor from England, on his first arrival, conducted himself with a kind of hauteur and superiority towards his sister and relations, but which was much heightened towards his acquaintance and countrymen in general;--there he was quite the man of consequence. He declared, with a magisterial air, that he should no longer permit them to fight, and cut one another's throats, as they had donet; that he should introduce peace among them, and make them love each other. He desired, when they came to see him at the Governor's, that they would be more cleanly in their persons, and less brutal in their manners. He was much offended at some little indelicacies which he observed in his sister, who came in such haste to see him, with his little nephew at her back, that she left all her paraphernalia behind her, and literally appeared in her birth-day suit.

Bannalong had not travelled for nothing; on the contrary, he had been an attentive observer of English manners, and particularly conducted himself with great propriety at table. His dress was also one of his primary concerns; and it was conjectured that he would not very readily renounce the comforts of a civilized life, to resume the precarious existence of a wandering savage. Immediately on his arrival, he made enquiries after his wife Goroobarrooboolo, whom he found cohabiting with Caruey. On presenting her with a smart gipsey hat, and a rose--coloured petticoat and jacket, she made no scruple of quitting her present lover, and returning to her quondam husband. In a few days, however, she evinced the inconsistency of her nature; for she was seen stripped of her finery, and walking totally unincumbered of all kind of cloathing.

Bannalong was also missing; Caruey was sought after, but he was not in the settlement; a few days developed the mystery, and we heard that he had been severely beaten by Bannalong, who availed himself of some lessons which he had acquired in England, and took his revenge, a-la Mendoza, to the great annoyance of poor Caruey, who had much rather met him with the weapons of the country, the club and the spear: However, he being much younger and handsomer than the victor, the lady once more changed her mind, and was resolved to follow the fortunes of Caruey. Bannalong seemed perfectly satisfied with the beating he had given his rival, and hinted that it was not worth his while to think about the lady, but that he should look out and make a better choice.

Bannalong soon became weary of the restraint he was under at the Governor's, and frequently absented himself, and went among his former associates for days and weeks together; always taking care to leave his cloaths behind him and to resume them when he re-appeared before the Governor. He continued these savage excursions for about three months, when a violent quarrel arose between him and his friend Coalby; a combat ensued, in which he got so much the worst of it, that he could not appear before the Governor till his wounds were healed. He acquainted his Excellency of the misunderstanding, and humbly requested that his clothes might be sent him, as also some provisions, of which he was greatly in want.

On his return to the settlement, his countenance was much disfigured; he had a wound on his mouth, which divided the upper lip, and broke two of the teeth, which gave a disgusting appearance to his face, and entirely altered his tone of voice. The source of his quarrel with Coalby was as follows: Finding himself indifferently received among the females, who did not much relish his European attainments, and not being able to gain a partner to his mind by fair means, he made an attack upon his friend's favourite, Booreea, in which he was not only unsuccessful, but was punished for his breach of friendship by Coalby, who sarcastically asked him if that conduct was a specimen of English manners.

There being among the more decent class of prisoners, several who were theatrically inclined, and being found to possess some merit, the Governor acceded to the petition of Mr. Sparrow, for permission to build a Theatre, which was accordingly completed on a very short time, at the expence of about one hundred pounds sterling; and it was opened, under his management, on Saturday the 16th of January, 1796, with Dr. Young's tragedy of The Revenge, which was performed in a much more respectable stile than could be expected. The house was fitted up with some taste, and the dresses were by no means despicable. In their license it was stated, that the slightest impropriety would be noticed, and the indulgence now granted immediately with-held. There was, however, more irregularity to be apprehended from some of the audience than from the players. The gallery was the largest part of the house, the nominal admission to which was one shilling, the payment produced an evil which was not foreseen, nor could well be prevented; for, in lieu of a shilling, as much flour, wheat, or spirits, as the manager thought proper to commute for the same, was often paid at the gallery door. It was feared that this, like gaming, would furnish another inducement to rob; and some of the most notorious of the convicts, ever on the watch to exercise their talents for depredation, looked upon the play-house as a grand desideratum, not by robbing the persons of the audience of their purses or their watches, but by breaking into their houses while the whole family were at the play; and this actually happened on the second night of their performing.

This was not the first theatrical essay; on his Majesty's Birth day, 1789, a party of the convicts performed the comedy of the Recruiting Officer, in a hut fitted up for the purpose; but the then infant state of the colony was unpropitious, and would not afford sufficient leisure for the colonists to indulge in a regular series of theatrical entertainments.

A soldier, of the name of Eades, much respected in the colony, in collecting thatch to cover a hut, which he had just built for the comfort of his family, overreaching himself, fell from a rock into the river, and was unfortunately drowned, leaving a wife and four children to bewail his loss; whereupon the players, with a liberality which reflected great credit upon them, performed the tragedy of the Fair Penitent, with a farce, for the benefit of the widow and orphans. The house was crowded, and the receipts amounted to near twenty pounds.

On the 18th of February, Mr. Muir found means to leave the colony, on board the Otter, bound for the N. W. coast of America. He left behind him a letter, in which he declared that he did not mean to infringe the laws of his country, by withdrawing himself from the colony, to return to any part of Great Britain, but that he should endeavour to get to America, and there to practise at the bar as an advocate, till his sentence should expire, when he should return to his native country. Here he chiefly passed his time in literary retirement, at a small pleasant house he had purchased, just without the town.

Notwithstanding the frequent attacks and depredations of the natives in the neighbourhood of Hawkesbury River, and when it was natural to suppose that self-preservation would have prompted the settlers to unite for their mutual defence, they seldom or ever evinced the smallest disposition to assist each other. This disposition being reported to the Governor, he issued a public order, directing that all people residing in the different settlements should, on the first alarm, immediately repair to the assistance of the persons attacked; and if it should be hereafter proved that any person or persons withheld their assistance, upon any attack of the natives, that they should be prosecuted, and punished accordingly. At the same time, such as had fire-arms were strictly enjoined not to fire at the natives on any account, but in their own defence, or that of their neighbours. It had been intimated to the Governor, that the two white men (Wilson and Knight) had been frequently seen with the natives in their excursions, and were supposed to direct and assist in the acts of hostility by which the settlers had lately suffered. He therefore ordered them to be looked after, and apprehended as soon as they were met with. These fellows were the occasion of the most serious mischief, exhorting the natives not to fear us, and showing them the inutility of our guns when once discharged, which soon removed that terror fire arms were wont to occasion.

The crime of forgery was now introduced into the colony. A shop being opened for the disposal of various articles imported in the store--ships, & c. and as orders on any of the officers, or responsible people, were taken, the prisoners practised their ingenuity, not only in counterfeiting dollars and rupees, but absolutely forged drafts and notes. One forged note for ten guineas, with the Commissary's name, was passed, but fortunately discovered. The offenders were committed for trial, but not a stiver's worth of the property was recovered.

In spite of every precaution that could be devised by Government, robberies still continued to encrease. Captain Paterson's premises were broken into, and a large property stolen from thence; a centinel was stationed at the door, yet the thieves had the address to make a hole in the wall at the back part of the building, through which they conveyed the articles. Captain Townson's house was entered the following night, and sixty pounds, in dollars and other property, were taken away. His servants were suspected, as were Captain Paterson's, but nothing could be proved upon them sufficient to warrant their apprehension.

Street robberies were frequently committed. On the feast of St. Patrick, two fellows, Matthew Farrell, and Richard Sutton (nick-named the Newgate Bully,) had the audacity to a ault the night watch, on being detected in the act of breaking into a house.

A criminal court being held in April, four prisoners were tried for forgery, when James M'Carthy was capitally convicted, and received sentence of death; the three others were acquitted. Other prisoners were tried for plundering the stores, one of whom was found guilty, viz. James Ashford, a lad, who had formerly been drummed out of the military corps: He was sentenced to seven years hard labour at Norfolk Island. A soldier was accused by an old man, a settler at the river, of an unnatural crime, but was acquitted. Two people of the stores were found guilty of stealing geese, the property of Mr. Grimes, and sentenced to receive corporal punishment. Another, in the same station, was sentenced to receive eight hundred lashes; and one man, George Hyson, for an attempt to commit the abominable crime of bestiality, was sentenced to stand in the pillory three times, an hour each time, and receive 900 lashes.

Daily experience proved, that those people whose sentences had expired were much greater evils than the other convicts. As no man was at this time spared from the public works, the shortest absence was noticed, and therefore we were well assured that the depredations and thefts were the handyworks of the former gentry, and their information was generally so accurate, that they never attempted a house that was not an object of plunder; and wherever there was any property, it was ten to one but they paid it a visit. It was suspected that the domestics of the house must have aided and assisted in these robberies, for the rogues always knew where to lay their hands on the property, and it was observed that they never once attempted the house of a poor individual.

There were also an amphibious kind of gentry, whose speculations were not confined to Terra Firma; for few ships that entered the harbour sailed from thence without receiving proofs of their address and ingenuity. It behoved the officers of every ship to keep the strictest guard over the people whom they permitted to come on board; for it was very obvious that every ship was visited by certain characters, to observe what kind of look-out they kept; many instances of this kind occurred, although one might have supposed a stranger would have been upon his guard, knowing what kind of people they were going to admit as visitors. A large quantity of tobacco had been stolen from the Bellona store-ship; half a barrel of gun-powder out of the Britannia, at the very time the master was entertaining some gentlemen from the settlement in the cabin. Mr. Page, the master of the Hope, was robbed of several articles, and the buckles out of his shoes, which were underneath his cot, wherein he lay asleep in the cabin; and a bale of goods from the Experiment; with an infinity of petty thefts of all descriptions.

In order to guard against this evil, it is necessary that masters should attend to something like the following rules:--Never to permit strangers to come on board without a certificate of leave; when on board, to be careful not to suffer them to go below, nor to see where any of the stores are stowed; never to permit a boat to come along-side in the night, unless there should be an officer in her; in that case, to make the boat push off, and lay upon her oars till his business was finished, when they should be called along-side to take him in. By these precautions, the greater part of these pilferings might be prevented. The decks of the ships at present are thronged with convicts, oftentimes of the most notorious characters in the colony.

On the 4th of July, a seaman was shot at Sydney by a convict; and, on the same day, John Fenlow, a settler at the river, shot his servant. Fenlow and the convict were taken into custody, and were ordered to be brought to immediate trial; but through the carelessness of the jailor, Fenlow, though encumbered with heavy irons, found means to make his escape from the cells, and was not retaken for near a month, when some of the natives discovered him lurking near his own habitation at the river, and giving information thereof, he was apprehended, and properly secured.

A criminal court of judicature being assembled early in the month of August, the following offenders were brought to trial:--Four convicts, for a burglary in the house of William Miller, but who, through a defect in the evidence, were acquitted. David Lloyd was tried for the wilful murder of John Smith, a seaman; it appeared that the seaman had gone to the house of Mr. Payne, the prisoner's master, in a state of intoxication, for the purpose of taking away, from a female convict-servant belonging to Mr. Payne, with whom the sailor cohabited during their passage, some clothes which he had given her. A riot, the natural consequence of such a proceeding, immediately ensued; and the prisoner endeavoured to make it appear that he had been compelled, in his own defence, to fire the pistol at the seaman. The court admitted that the prisoner had not any malice against the deceased, which was necessary to constitute the crime of murder; and therefore found him guilty of manslaughter, and sentenced him to receive six hundred lashes.--John Fenlow, for the wilful murder of his servant, David Lane; this charge was fully proved, and the prisoner received sentence of death. Farrell, who, with Sutton, the Newgate Bully, assaulted the watch on St. Patrick's Day last, when the latter received a wound on the temple, of which he languished and died: the watchmen were now brought up to account for his death; this they did to the satisfaction of the court, and were discharged. Four vagabonds, who had repeatedly broken out of prison, and ran away from the jail gang--a party, who, from being hardened and notorious offenders, were kept at work in irons, and when the labour of the day was over, were locked up in the prison till they returned to their daily task--were tried as incorrigible rogues, and sentenced to three years hard labour in Norfolk Island, which being so small, they could not so easily elude the vigilance of the overseers. One man was tried for a rape, but acquitted. Fenlow was tried on the Saturday, and executed on the following Monday, and his body was delivered to the surgeons for dissection. It could scarcely be supposed that curiosity would have prevailed so strong, in a society composed as this is; for it was no sooner signified by the surgeons that the body was ready for inspection, than the hospital was crowded with men, women, and children, to the number of several hundreds, none of whom seemed, in the smallest degree, to betray any horror or concern at the dreadful spectacle before them.

In consequence of these enormities, several judicious regulations were made. All persons who had been struck off the stores, and of course did not labour for the public, were ordered forthwith to appear at Sydney, in order to their being mustered, and examined relative to their respective terms of transportation; when certificates were to be given to such as were regularly discharged from the Commissary's books, and the settlers were directed not to employ any but such as could produce this certificate. Frequent visits were to be made by the magistrates, for the purpose of settling such differences as might arise among the settlers and other persons; and the Governor declared that he would himself inspect their conduct from time to time, and severely punish those who held his orders in contempt, by affording shelter and encouragement to the thieves and vagabonds who were rambling up and down the country.

These regulations were made as public as possible; and there being a printing-press in the settlement, under the management of one Hughes, large bills of the proclamation were printed, and dispersed throughout the different districts, that none might plead ignorance; and the town of Sydney was soon filled with people from the surrounding settlements, who came to the Judge-Advocate for certificates of their having served their terms, agreeably to their respective sentences. Among these were many who had been absent a long time, and whose terms were yet unexpired; some who had escaped from prison, and others who were for life, had changed their names, in order to impose on the officers. By the activity of the overseers, and a strict investigation of the necessary books and papers, they were in general detected in the imposition, and were sent to hard labour in the jail gang, which now encreased in numbers every day. Two notorious offenders, Luke Normington and Richard Elliott, were detected in robbing the Commissary's stock-yard. These were sent to the jail-gangs; also one Sharpless, a convict, who, after marrying the most deformed and ugly woman in the whole colony, took it into his head to be jealous of her, and gave her so dreadful a beating, that her life was in the utmost danger.

The colony now began to assume the appearance of being able to supply itself with respect to the necessaries of life, there being near six thousand acres of land in cultivation, and all the stores abundantly filled. In the houses of individuals were to be found most of the comforts, and not a few of the luxuries of life, for which we were indebted to our intercourse with India; and our early years of toil, famine, and difficulty, were now exchanged for an aera of plenty, ease, and pleasure.

During this time, my domestic concerns improved imperceptibly, so that my situation was equal, if not preferable, to most of the settlers here; having a flock of sheep, consisting of thirty-eight, with fourteen goats, a most excellent milch cow, half a dozen breeding sows, and a very plentiful stock of poultry; and, to add to the comforts of my situation, in the month of September, 1796, his Excellency, Governor Hunter, was pleased to present me with an absolute pardon, under the great seal of the colony, and appointed me a principal superintendant of the district of Parramatta, with a permanent salary of fifty pounds a year, in the room of Mr. Thomas Clark, who was returning to England. Hitherto my situation had been only provisional. The Governor was pleased to compliment me on the "faithful discharge of my duty, the integrity and uniform uprightness of my conduct, and my general behaviour during my whole residence in the colony, which," he said, "perfectly obliterated every trace of my former indiscretions." It was such a friend as this to whom I alluded on a solemn occasion, previous to my leaving England;--this was the "generous and powerful man" I so much needed in my youthful days, to come forward and say, "Barrington, you have some abilities, which may be of service to yourself and the public--I feel for your situation, and will place you in a condition to try the sincerity of your intentions; and as long as you act with diligence and integrity, you shall not want for "countenance and relief." The above flattering eulogiums of his excellency, Governor Hunter, the station I fill, and the consideration and friendship I exprience from the most respectable persons in the colony, prove that, in my address to Baron Eyre, I was ingenuous and sincere.

THE END